Dogs Talk

Also by Adrian Doyle

This Smallholding Life

Dogs Talk
Four Dogs Tell Their Stories

Adrian Doyle

First published in Great Britain in 2020

Paperback ISBN: 978-1-8380010-2-5
eBook ISBN: 978-1-8380010-3-2

Find out more about Adrian and Nicole, their
smallholding and shop here:
www.auchenstroan.com

Editorial services by
www.bookeditingservices.co.uk

To Nicole

"Before I left, I tried one more time to explain that dogs needed to be treated as dogs and that the best way to turn them into good pets was through the application of dog psychology. Understand the dogs' needs and then put in place measures to satisfy those needs and you will have a happy, obedient dog. However, I was not convinced that they believed me."

CONTENTS

Preface...i

Maxibon 1

George...45

Kika 99

Haribo..153

Case Studies 169

Glossary 196

Preface

This book is a set of stories told by four dogs and how they coped when they found themselves living with a dog psychologist. Each dog had their own set of issues, each unique to the dog yet common across dogs worldwide.

The Author

I have always felt that I've had a connection with animals. Indeed, my ambition as a youngster was to become a vet – an ambition quashed by some dubious (in retrospect) parental advice. In my dream of being a vet, I would be stationed overseas (probably Africa) in a large animal sanctuary or reserve dealing with animals such as lions, elephants and buffalo. The parental advice ran along the lines that I'd be clipping budgies' teeth for the rest of my life. I ended up working in information technology.

Nevertheless, animals continued to play an important part of my life, mainly through my wildlife gardens. I have built a lot of habitats and ponds over the years. I have also been active in various conservation charities as well as helping hedgehogs through the winter for decades now.

I only started keeping dogs once I left corporate life. The first was a German shepherd rescued from Battersea

Dogs Home, Egham. He was a bit of a handful, so I started reading up on dogs. One book led to another, and I started to get an instinctive feel for how to understand dogs and their behaviour. German shepherds are pretty easy dogs, really, once you get to know how they think.

Over the years, I continued to learn what I could, and was particularly inspired by Cesar Milan and his TV programmes. His approach of using dog psychology chimed strongly with what I had learnt. As well as working with my own dogs, as featured in this book, I also helped out at rescue centres and worked for a while at an excellent dog boarding facility. There, my job was to watch over the dogs as they played in a field. It was intensely satisfying keeping the dogs happy, intercepting trouble before it started and generally earning the trust of so many dogs in a pretty short amount of time.

Word got around about my ability with the dogs. In turn, this led to me working as a dog behaviour specialist. I have included a selection of case studies at the end of this book which summarise some of my work in that area.

One thing I found is that I spent a lot of time as human counsellor when working with problem dogs. I have also trained and practised as a therapist specialising in clinical hypnotherapy. A number of dogs I went to see had problems stemming from issues in their owners' lives. Unbeknown to the owners, these human issues were often at the root of the dogs' problems. With some clients, I spent more time working with the owner than the dog.

I continue to learn about dogs through books, occasional TV programmes and also by just observing dogs and how they interact. George and Haribo, two of the dogs featured in this book, still have plenty to teach me.

Dog Psychology

A dog psychologist is not a dog therapist. They don't sit the dog on a couch and listen to its problems. What a dog psychologist does is understand how dogs think. Combining this understanding with breed characteristics, dog psychologists can work out how dogs perceive and react to human actions. Essentially, they can interpret dog behaviours from the dog, rather than the human perspective. This means they can work out effective ways to change dog behaviours that make sense to the dog.

This dog perception of humans can be quite different from what we humans might think. For example, dogs ignore each other as a matter of course. In the human world, ignoring another human is perceived as rude behaviour. By projecting human social norms onto dogs, we can all too easily worry, unnecessarily, when we see our dog ignoring another dog or even another human.

There is also a huge social pressure on humans to pander to dogs even when ignoring them might be the better course of action. Many people have asked me if I don't like dogs because I have ignored their pooch as it has jumped all over me trying to get my attention when I pass through their front door. They then seem surprised when the dog calms down pretty quickly and I explain that I was having a conversation with their dog and actually just establishing some rules.

Also, knowing what to do when two clearly unbalanced German shepherds have escaped their leads and are charging towards you with intent can be useful. A typical human response might be to look at them and try to greet them with a "good dog". That's the last thing you should try. The correct response is to turn away slightly and pretend they don't exist. This works for a number of reasons. First, if you make eye contact with a guard dog, it will interpret that as a challenge. Had I looked at these approaching dogs, I would have, in their eyes, changed from an object of interest to a potential threat. By looking away, I avoided this. Second, by turning away, I was, in dog "language", stating that I wasn't backing down but I didn't wish to fight. Note, I just turned away about 45 degrees. Turning my back on them would also have been a mistake, as I could have been interpreted as prey. Finally, I remained completely calm and relaxed. Dogs can sense our moods and by remaining relaxed, I was signalling I was not a threat.

When these two dogs arrived at my feet and found me observing the sky, they didn't know what to do. They stopped and looked around at their owner for instructions.

Another example of miscommunication between humans and dogs is comforting. It is human instinct to comfort a person or animal in distress. However, with dogs, inappropriate comforting can sometimes have the opposite effect, such as reinforcing fears and phobias. This is particularly true with anxious dogs.

It's worth noting that the vast majority of dog behaviour issues are learnt. That is to say, the dogs have learnt them from humans. Dogs are not born yappy. They are not born with a fear of cars, cyclists, bangs, other dogs, thunder and lightning, and so on.

This brings to mind a discussion I had with a client who countered by telling me that horses are terrified of fireworks. This is true, but it highlights another problem faced by dogs. We humans class animals as animals, and make comparisons and connections that we shouldn't. Horses are prey animals. A sudden and unexpected noise could signify a threat. It could be a predator closing in. In this situation, the horse's fight or flight response kicks in. It will have an adrenaline rush. If it cannot fight or run away, for example it's in a stable, it will panic.

A dog is a predator animal. A sudden noise might be of

interest but would not necessarily be perceived as a threat. If the noise were to turn into something that hurt the dog, it would be remembered as a threat. If the noise were, however, just the noise but then nothing happened, the dog would ignore it. Fear of noises is learnt from human actions.

There are many books that deal with dog behaviour. The ones I have read are told from the human perception. This book attempts to tell the stories from the dog's perspective. While that carries a risk of anthropomorphism, I have done my best not to fall into that trap. The dogs tell their stories by telling events as they would interpret them, but they are explained in a way a human can understand. My apologies if I have got it wrong in places.

Dogs and Humans

The relationship between dogs and humans goes back centuries. Over that time, humans have, through selective breeding, created a range of different breeds of dogs with different skill sets. The original dog, the wolf, is a good general all-rounder. Wolves are well known for their stamina. They can follow prey for miles until the prey animal becomes too tired to escape. They can also sprint quickly when needed. They have an excellent sense of smell, excellent hearing and good eyesight. They have also been observed working as a team to round up prey and move it towards a trap.

Modern, specialised breeds have often focused on improving specific skills, such as a better sense of smell (hounds), speed (sighthounds), protective instincts (guard dogs), rounding up livestock (shepherd dogs), pulling loads (huskies and mastiffs), and so on. These are generally classed as working dogs. It should be noted that by increasing skills in one area, dogs' skills are decreased in other areas. For example, improving smell might lead to poorer eyesight.

Selective breeding is a fairly recent thing and seems to have reached a peak in the 19th century. Reading through the history of dog breeding, it almost seems as though each and every landowner created a breed either to do a job, as a hobby or even to gain the breeder recognition. The result is that there is a vast range of dog breeds. Even within each type of breed, there are many variations. If we look at the terrier, for example, we find that there are around 35 breeds: Border terriers, West Highland terriers, bull terriers, Airedales, the list goes on. In fact, there are so many that some iconic breeds are now endangered. The West Highland terrier of Greyfriars Bobby fame is one such breed.

Up until relatively recently (mid to late 20th century), most dogs were kept as working dogs. Collies rounded up sheep. Mastiffs and huskies pulled carts and sleds. German shepherds, Rottweilers and Dobermans stood as guard dogs. Terriers were used for vermin control. Many breeds also supported hunting activities.

These days, many dogs are kept as house pets. Often, these dogs do not get their breed needs fulfilled, and this can lead to behavioural issues for the dogs. Also, many dogs are now treated as part of a human family. This is difficult for dogs because they think differently from humans. They are first and foremost dogs. Their needs are quite specific and, if not met, can cause problems for the dog. This, in turn, can cause problems for the owner.

In fact, in my opinion the biggest challenge faced by the modern pet dog is in meeting the needs of its owner. Most pet dog owners get dogs to satisfy a human need of some sort. This may be companionship, need for exercise or simply that the family has always kept dogs. Many owners do little or no research into the needs of the animal they have acquired. Contrast this with other types of pets. Keeping fish, for example, requires specialist knowledge about water, tanks, filters, food, and so on. If you don't know what you are doing, the fish soon die. The same can be said for many types of pets, particularly exotic pets such as snakes and lizards.

Dogs, however, are adaptable and muddle through to the best of their abilities. It is quite easy for humans to ignore or not even see a dog's issues until it is too late. Usually, too late means something has been attacked and maybe even died. This could be anything from a garden bird to a person!

A common issue is livestock. Owners, in their ignorance (or even wishful thinking that their dog is "perfect"), walk through fields with sheep. They let their dog off the lead, and are then stunned or shocked when their dog hares off after the sheep, scaring and even killing them.

How many dog owners have read the Dangerous Dog Act?

The biggest challenge I face when working in dog rehabilitation is convincing owners that they are the root of their dog's problems. What this means is that I have to ask them to redefine their relationship with their dog. Ideally, they would put their dog's needs first rather than the other way around. While many seem to think that this is a good idea in principle, few achieve any change for the better. The problem here is that most dog owners believe they are meeting the needs of their dogs through fawning attention, treats, comfortable beds, access to sofas, and so on. In effect, they believe that treating a dog as a human is a step up for the dog, that it is better for the dog. They fundamentally cannot see that their behaviour is actually destructive from the dog's point of view.

Those who make the effort to see things from the dog's

point of view can achieve remarkable results.

A selection of case studies is provided at the end of the book that helps to illustrate this point.

One such case study was a family who had two English bull terriers that were tearing lumps out of each other. They were supposed to be keeping each other company. The dogs had to be kept apart at all times. They had cost the owner a fortune in vet bills. I worked out what was going on, explained it to the owners and showed them what to do, i.e. what to look for and when and how to intervene. These owners listened and changed their approach. Within a short time, we had the two dogs together in a room and all was calm.

It can be done, but it needs the humans to think about the dog's actual needs (as a dog) and put those first, not the other way around.

There are many books out there that describe dogs, how they think, what they need. Many are training manuals. Training is important, but the real key to understanding dogs is to understand their psychology. Knowing how dogs think can lead to a better relationship with your dog. It's not that different from human interpersonal relationships.

As I have mentioned, the approach in this book is to try and explain dog rehabilitation from a dog's perspective. It features the stories of four dogs. Each came to me with a specific set of issues. All were unbalanced in some way.

The Dogs in This Book

Maxibon, a small terrier from Spain, was like a teddy bear, until you tried to get her to do something she didn't want to do. If you went near her food, she'd have your fingers. She had also developed a range of fears, including thunder, fireworks and, of all things, cattle grids. She was my soon-to-be wife's dog, so I had to tread carefully.

George, an Anatolian shepherd, came to us in pretty much a feral state. Rescued as a puppy in Greece, he was only one year old. However, already, he had been returned to rescue centres many times, even by experienced dog owners. It seemed that no one could cope with him. He was recommended to me by a dog rescue centre where I volunteered. I like big dogs, but even I was unprepared for George.

Kika, another Spanish dog, lived with us for a few weeks while her owner was in hospital. She was one of the most badly behaved dogs I have ever met. Aside from marking the floors inside the house, she was uncontrollable outside and aggressive to any other dog that came within 50 metres. Kika's was the first story to be written. Knowing there was a risk that her owner would undo everything, we hit upon the idea of Kika keeping a diary. The idea was that her owner would enjoy reading the diary and maybe change the way she interacted with Kika. This is why Kika's story is written in chronological order.

Haribo, a tricolour collie, came to us with two typewritten pages of issues. His was also a history of rejection. He was more or less abandoned at a dog centre where I worked. He had to be muzzled around other dogs. We took him in as his owner was clearly trying to rehome him to anyone who would take him.

Of all the dogs, Haribo's story is the shortest. I read the list of issues and threw it in the bin. To be honest, aside from an underlying anxiety, there were only two issues causing any real problems. One was a propensity to raid the kitchen bin. The other was a deep-rooted fear aggression towards other dogs. While I would like to take credit for turning Haribo around, I actually think the real credit lies with George. He was Haribo's true mentor.

Haribo dotes on George and has learnt so much from

him. I think George provided and continues to provide the stability that Haribo needs far more ably than any human could. It's also worth mentioning that being a collie, it is in Haribo's instinct to follow human commands. In essence, he likes to do what he is told and thrives on being given something to so. The other three are independent breeds used to thinking for themselves.

These dogs' stories try to highlight their rehabilitation from their point of view. It tries to show some of the difficulties we humans have when dealing with dogs. Our human intentions may be clear to us, but they can mean something entirely different to a dog.

My approach to dogs has been inspired by many, but the names that stick in my mind are Bruce Fogle, Cesar Milan and Stanley Coren. All three have published excellent books.

Maxibon

Maxibon

I'm Maxibon (Maxi for short) and this is my story. I was born in Spain. I am a small dog, about the same size as a miniature poodle. You know, bigger than a lapdog but maybe half the size of a small collie. I am covered in light brown curly fur. On a human, my fur might look like a 1970s perm. I also have big eyes, deep as pools, which I can make even bigger when I want something.

My first memory is as a tiny puppy a few weeks old. I had been tied to a post and left on my own. That didn't last long; I soon chewed through the rope and headed off down the road. I was picked up by a random human and taken back to their house. I was only there a few days before I was taken to a new home where I met a new human called Nicole. I liked Nicole straight away – she fed me, gave me a place to sleep and generally doted on me. I loved that – nothing quite like a bit of doting from a human. Well, nothing like a LOT of doting from a human, truth be told.

I am a mongrel but mostly terrier, and come with all the habits and instincts of that breed. We are known for being fearless. Any dog, any size, any time, I reckon I could have it for breakfast. I am not sure if it's true that we are brave, because I thought you had to overcome fear to be brave. What's fear? As I said, we terriers are fearless. We are also energetic, active and playful. We can be quite a handful, especially when we are young. We will be charging around, running off – just basically having fun, fun and more fun.

Most of all, we are independent and smart. We like to make our own minds up. Well, I certainly do. Dog training? Good luck with that. I'll sit if I want to, not because some human tells me to. That might make us terriers sound a bit arrogant. Not at all. We are sweet little dogs who love attention (when it suits us) and we make great "pets". I say "pets" in inverted commas because we're not really the pets – it's the humans who are the pets. At least that's what we terriers like to think.

It wasn't long before I had my pet human well trained. Only the best food for me. The most comfortable part of the couch was all mine. On our walks, I'd leave my human to wait for me and head off down the beach looking for playmates. Sometimes I could hear my human barking at me. I'm not sure what that was all about. To be honest, I was a bit miffed she'd moved from where I left her without checking with me first. Anyway, once I was played out, I'd scamper back to my pet human and we'd head home. Then it would be a nice snooze for me.

I liked where we lived; there were places I could crawl under and have a quiet nap. I have always liked that, crawling under places. Be it a human bed, a sofa or long grass, I can make myself nice and comfortable and have a lovely wee sleep.

We got on great, my human and me. She called me Maxibon, Maxi for short, but my nickname was Peluche. That's Spanish for "teddy bear" in case you didn't know.

One day everything changed. We left Spain and headed to a much cooler place called England. I am not sure why. I didn't get to travel with my pet human. I was most perturbed that I had to go separately. I'll be honest, I didn't know what to make of the journey as I spent a lot of time trapped in a small space. But, thankfully, the journey ended and there she was, waiting for me in this cold and chilly land. Good job I am a ball of fluff or I might have got a bit cold!

There were two amazing things about England, though: grass and squirrels. Grass, how can I begin to describe it? Cool and soft – it was a lovely sensation to roll about on it feeling the texture through my fur. And the smell – rich, warm and tangy. It brought a lovely tingle to my nose. I had never smelt anything like that green grass. Every time we went for a walk, there was all this green grass everywhere. What can a dog do? I rolled about in it. In fact, I rolled and rolled and rolled and rolled. My humans could get quite impatient. But they had to wait; there was nothing quite like grass rolling.

Nothing like grass rolling except for chasing squirrels. I had never seen a squirrel before I came to England. Small furry creatures with big fluffy tails just perfect for chasing. If I caught scent of one of those, I was off. Nothing would stop me. Again, my humans seemed a bit put out by this. I never understood why. They brought me here. In fact, the real question is why were the humans not chasing squirrels?

Anyway, my human introduced me to the rest of her pack. There was Liz, Harry and Matt. It wasn't long before I had all of them eating out of my paws. So, cold and rainy days aside, life in England was good. I did what I wanted when I wanted and generally wound the humans around my little toe.

Occasionally, the humans would make me do something I didn't really like, such as go for a walk late at night. One minute I was cosy and fast asleep, and the next minute I was dragged out into the cold. And they would keep me there till I did a wee, even if I didn't really need one. Mind you, once I was out, I did quite enjoy sniffing around.

Life was good, I mean, I developed a fear of storms, but they are loud and scary, so there's nothing wrong with that. OK, so when I got scared, I'd go into a manic state and trash the room. But what was wrong with that? I also became a very fussy eater. Well, you are what you eat, are you not? I'd only eat the best food and only when I felt like it. My humans seemed to eat at set times, but for me it was food on demand. Yes, OK, if I got bored, I'd just wander off on my own looking for adventure. But that's what we dogs like to do. And if I didn't get my way, I'd sit, tremble and pant until I did. It was very effective; I always got my way in the end.

Everything was just as I wanted it, or so I thought. Then, I met Adrian.

First Contact

At that time, I lived in my flat with two humans. I had my human, Nicole, and her brother, Matt. From time to time, I would stay around at my nan's, Nicole's mother. I had all three just where I wanted them.

Nicole fed me the best meat she could find. I ate it as and when I felt like it. I felt like I was the queen of my small domain. It was all perfect. Yes, I mean, I know I had developed a few issues over time. There was my fear of thunderstorms that I've already mentioned – well, any loud bang really. I panted and trembled for all I was worth if I didn't get my way. I'd go mad if the car went over a cattle grid. I'd get quite annoyed if I wasn't given food from the humans' table. Nothing to worry about really. Other than those little things, I was just about perfect.

One day, Nicole went and got a new boyfriend. I knew this because I could catch traces of his scent on Nicole's clothes. One day, she brought him home. His name was Adrian. As he came through the front door, I put on my best teddy bear face and rushed across. I jumped up on my back legs to make sure he could see me. I was more excited than I can describe.

The thing was, he just ignored me. I jumped and jumped and jumped, but nothing. He just walked past, chatting to my humans. I watched, incredulous. I tried one more time to get his attention, but he just blanked me. *OK*, I thought, *I get it*. I believe humans find it rude, but we dogs are quite happy to ignore one another. It's part of our language. On a first meeting like this, a high-status dog will totally blank a lower-status dog. Perfectly normal behaviour. For a dog! Adrian, a human, was telling me that he was a higher-status dog than me.

But that was the nub of the problem. I was the high-status dog in my flat. As I have already said, I was queen of this domain. If any dog was doing the ignoring, it should have been me. So, I stopped my jumping up, replaced my teddy bear face with a textbook scowl, and went and jumped on the sofa.

This was an unusual experience for me. Most humans were besotted with me in seconds. I don't remember if any had ignored me, ever. *Oh well*, I thought, *he'll soon fall into line in my pack*. At that, I dozed off. Later on, he did pay me some attention. By then, I was stretched out on the floor happily in my own world. I made a mental note of this. Jumping up got me no attention from Adrian. However, when I was completely relaxed, he would come over and stroke my head gently – the kind of attention I liked.

All was fine until bedtime. I can tell when my humans are heading for bed. This is not difficult – they head for the bedroom and go through their bedtime ritual. That evening, at bedtime, I jumped up onto Nicole's bed, as was my custom. I also had my own night-time routine. I had my own basket in the hallway, but I preferred to sleep on top of or underneath my humans' beds. During the night, I'd start by sleeping on top of Nicole's bed, and then later I'd move under the bed. Later still, I'd move under Matt's bed. Sometimes, I'd sleep on the sofa or in my basket for a while. My routine was kind of fluid.

That night, there I was lying curled up at the end of the bed when I felt a human hand on my back. It was the male human, the new boyfriend, Adrian, pushing me off the bed. Let me repeat that, he was PUSHING ME OFF THE BED! I wasn't having that. I growled my most menacing growl. When that didn't work, I tried to bite his hand. He must have been expecting that because I missed with my snapping jaws – and I'm pretty fast. I found myself standing on the floor. To be honest, I was both surprised and perplexed.

This wasn't on. This was my flat and this was my bed. I jumped straight back up. Adrian was waiting for me. I found my path blocked, and once again I was standing on the floor. I looked up. Adrian was sitting on the end of the bed looking at me. It occurred to me that he was very calm. There was no malice there. He didn't want to fight; he just wanted me to know that he owned the bed now. I could tell from his body language that he meant it.

I wasn't sure what to make of this. Adrian's grasp of dog communication had surprised me. He was kind of acting like a dog pack leader. In my house. Leading my pack. I hadn't encountered a human acting as a dog pack leader before, and I wasn't sure what to do. I mean, I got all of this, but I wasn't happy. For a few seconds I stood there, bemused. It was as though my brain had stopped. Nothing happened. Adrian just sat there watching me. I decided to back down and headed to my next favourite place, under the bed, where I lay down and went to sleep.

Barking at the Table

By now, I was also visiting Adrian's house and sometimes even staying over. I began to notice that things were a little bit different here. For example, I wasn't allowed onto the sofa. That didn't stop me trying, though. I mean, it was comfortable and I still considered myself top dog. Yes, it was Adrian's house, but now that I had been there, I considered it to be no more than an extension to my own territory.

My house, my sofa.

However, every time I jumped up onto the sofa, I was immediately moved off it. It was most perplexing. That said, I never jumped up on the bed here. I had conceded that all of the human beds were Adrian's territory. I was quite happy to sleep on the cushions left on the floor for me. To be honest, I also quite liked sleeping at the top of the stairs.

Anyway, all was calm until dinner time.

Since Nicole had adopted me, I have always been able to go where I wanted. One of the places I liked to be was under the dinner table where the humans ate. Human dinner meant titbit time. In the wild, the higher-status dogs eat first and as the highest-status dog in the pack, I would duly expect to get my share straight away. It's not as if I needed the food. Nicole fed me the best bits of high-quality meat and if I didn't eat it there and then, it was left out so I could finish it later. I could eat any time I felt like it.

That wouldn't happen in the wild. If a pack of dogs made a kill, it would be scoffed pretty quickly. There was always the risk something bigger (like another dog) might come along and snatch it. In domesticity, we dogs are not known for respecting other dogs' food bowls. Put food down in front of more than one dog and, without supervision or a well-structured pack, we can start fighting over it.

But, for me, I could eat as and when I liked. What this meant was that I could leave my food till after the humans' meal time. That way, I could eat the food from the table and then, if I felt like it, I could eat some of my food. It was a pretty good life being queen dog.

So, it was human dinner time and I took my place under the table and waited. I was pretty sure I had my humans well trained by now. If I didn't get my share quickly enough, I'd bark at the humans to remind them of their duty. I. Want. Food. Now. That said, because I had my humans so well trained, I rarely had to bark.

So, there I was, under the table at Adrian's house waiting for my share. No food was proffered, so I barked. To hammer the message home, I sat upright and stared straight at Adrian to demonstrate my dominance. I barked using single barks. However, despite the barking, which had always worked before, no food was forthcoming. In fact, the humans were ignoring me. I could sense Nicole being a little anxious at this. Quite – she knew her place. Where was my share? I carried on barking and adjusting my sit position so that they had to see me.

All of a sudden, I was shepherded out of the room. It all happened in a bit of a blur. Adrian had stood up and gently moved me out into the hallway using his feet and legs. I was so surprised I even forgot to growl or bite him. Well, I wasn't having that. I ran straight past him and under the table. Once again, I was hustled out of the dining room. This time, the door was shut on me. I couldn't believe it! How very dare he!

I started digging my way back in. The floor was made of concrete covered in carpet, but that wasn't going to stop me, I'm a terrier after all. The door opened and Adrian stood there looking down at me. He held my gaze and moved into my space forcing me to retreat a little. This was a new experience for me. Adrian was behaving like a dog. The eye contact and moving me out of my space were dominant dog behaviours. And, all the time, he was perfectly calm and non-threatening.

I retreated to the kitchen.

Adrian returned to the table and the humans carried on with their dinner. The dining room door was open but I felt, strangely, unable to go back into the dining room. Not sure what to do at this point, I headed into the living room and jumped on the sofa. Well, what did you expect? I had to re-exert my dominance somehow. Annoyingly, I wasn't there for long. I don't know how he knew I was on the sofa. I'm pretty sure I had not been seen. Nevertheless, Adrian appeared and moved me off. I jumped back up on it. This turned out to be a bad move because I then found myself locked in the kitchen. By now, I was in a bit of a mood.

Everything I'd tried had been blocked. Not only blocked, but in a way that avoided a dogfight. I still wasn't giving up. I tried to dig my way out of the kitchen. However, this proved fruitless as the floor was tiled.

Scratching at the door also failed to get any response. There was nothing left to do but wait, so I gave up and lay down. What was odd was that I felt something I had not felt for a long time. I felt calm, relaxed even. I liked it. While a human in a comparable situation might have sat there brooding, as a dog living in the moment I just accepted the situation. With my earlier mood having evaporated, I lay down and dozed off.

I awoke to find that the humans had finished their dinner. Adrian looked in on me, and I moved my eyes to look at him. He called me to follow, and we went into the living room. He patted a cushion on the floor, and I felt myself going onto it and lying down. How did he do that? Then he gave me some pats and quality attention. Nicole joined in. That was great.

The thing is, my usual tricks and behaviours were not working with Adrian. He refused to back down. He was acting like a dog – and a pack leader, to boot. But I was the pack leader, or so I thought. I found my respect for him growing. Normally, a change of leadership would come after a fight, but Adrian was exerting control in a way which avoided that. It was a new experience for me.

It seemed I would have to settle for being pack leader when Adrian was not around. I could still boss Nicole and my nan around.

Needless to say, I was never let near the table again. Paradoxically, I actually liked this, as I stopped worrying about table snacks. Overall, I found that I didn't feel as anxious when I was at Adrian's house. The structure suited me and I didn't have to make all the decisions – I could leave those up to Adrian.

I felt happier there.

Choking

I was beginning to notice subtle changes in my life now. These were mainly when we were over at Adrian's place. His pack rules were always enforced when he was around. I could sense, even from a dog's perspective, that Nicole was not always in agreement. That was fine with me; life at Nicole's and my nan's remained much as it always was. For me, it was something of a conundrum. I wanted to push back against the rules, to take back control, but at the same time, I liked the new structure. I also felt generally less anxious, but I wasn't sure why that was.

A big change to my routine was that my access to food was now restricted to mealtimes. I had to eat while the food was there, or I went hungry. To a human, that might sound harsh, but for me it was one less thing to worry about. When food is always there, there's always the temptation to nibble it. You can spend the day wondering do I eat or don't I eat. Now, I got fed at mealtimes and that was that. To be honest, it made life a bit easier. It also touched a deeper instinct, one that said eat when you can.

However, sometimes I would get a treat. These days this was usually linked to some sort of activity. Sometimes I had to do things like sit or lie down to get my treat. That was fun and I enjoyed it. This evening, however, we played what you might call "hide and seek". Nicole put me in a "sit" and showed me a treat. She had my undivided attention. Then she disappeared off upstairs somewhere. I had learnt to remain sitting when this happened, so that's what I did, and then Nicole duly reappeared. She no longer had the treat. She then said something like "find", which I had learnt meant that I could go and find the treat.

I headed upstairs searching for the treat. I loved this game. I had to sniff out all sorts of nooks and crannies in order to find it, but eventually I tracked it down. It was a chewy treat, and my next task was to find somewhere quiet to eat it. I stood there with treat in mouth and eyes blazing. There were no beds to crawl under in this house. What I mean is that there were beds but not enough space for me to get under them. Where should I go? I stood at the top of the landing looking down. There were no humans in sight. While I wanted a quiet corner, I also liked being close to the humans. So I bounced down the stairs, tiptoed across the hall and slunk into the living room. There was a space between the door, a wall and the sofa. It wasn't perfect, but it would do. I lay down and bit down on my treat. It was delicious and I was in doggie heaven.

As I moved it around my mouth to get a better bite on it, it got lodged between my teeth at the back of my mouth. It kind of made me choke a bit. I tried to loosen it but to no avail. It was a chewy treat and it had got well and truly stuck to my back teeth. I was a bit perturbed, more because I was not managing to eat the treat than being worried about it being stuck. Nicole heard me choking and came to see what was going on. Spotting the lodged treat, she reached down to take it.

I went mad. This was my treat and nobody was taking it away from me for any reason whatsoever. Nicole might think she owns me, but she is in no position to take my food. Despite having the troublesome treat lodged in my mouth, I growled and snapped at her hand and caught one of her fingers, drawing blood. I lay there snarling, challenging anyone to come close. I was ready for action. I was ready for full-on violence. Bring it on!

By now, Adrian had joined us and he stood looking down at me. I continued snarling and gave him my fiercest look. He may have acted as though he was pack leader, but he was not getting my treat. My teeth were bared and my warning growls were at their most menacing. Adrian said something in human to Nicole and then crouched down next to me. I snarled and snarled for all I was worth, but he didn't seem to be getting the message.

In fact, in a flash he had me pinned to the ground on my side. In this position, I couldn't reach round and bite him. Believe me, I tried really hard, wriggling and doing everything I could to claw my way out of there. They were not getting MY treat. Adrian just kept me pinned there, and I soon ran out of puff. It was quite hard doing all that snarling, especially with a treat making it a bit awkward to breath. I paused to gather my strength and in that moment, Adrian reached across and pinned my head to the floor. I was completely immobilised. I growled again and tried to wriggle free. If I could just get my claws into his arm, maybe I'd get free. While I was trying to do that, Nicole reached into my mouth and carefully removed the lodged treat.

As I was let free, I sprang to my feet in indignation. Both humans were now standing chatting amongst themselves as though nothing had happened. I was looking for my treat – where was it? I mean, it was nice not to have it jammed in my mouth, but I wanted to eat it now. Where was my treat? My humans wandered into the kitchen, and I followed. I could smell my treat but couldn't find it. I had a good look around but despite using my eyes and my nose, I couldn't find the treat. *Oh well*, I thought. My treat was gone and all around was calm. Not much I could do really. I lay down on the kitchen floor and went to sleep.

Forest Walks

One advantage of staying round at Adrian's place was that he had a garden – something we didn't have at my flat. On a good day (not raining), he'd leave the back door open, so I could wander in and out as I pleased. As I think I mentioned, I quite like the feel of grass on my back, and there was a small lawn where I could roll about on.

He also lived next to a forest, which meant forest walks.

The forest was quite popular with people and dogs, so there were usually lots of smells to check out.

In the past, I have always liked other dogs. As a puppy, I was a right little play dog. If I spotted another dog, I'd be straight over trying to get them to run around and play with me. These days, I was bit older, around 10 (human years) I think. While I still liked meeting other dogs, I wasn't up for running around and playing so much. I also liked my space. This meant that sometimes I had to tell dogs off for getting too close. Just a quick bark and maybe a small nip to the neck. Nothing much. I had to let them know who was boss and to make sure they kept their distance.

On walks with Nicole or my nan, I had a lot of freedom. Once we'd got to the park or woodland, I'd be let off the lead to go and do my own thing. This meant that I could run over to say hello when I saw another dog. Sometimes, as I have mentioned, I'd have to keep the other dog in its place. When this happened, I'd sometimes get told off by a human. I'm not sure why – I mean, my humans didn't speak dog, so they couldn't know what had happened between me and the other dog. Besides, I was in charge, so it was up to me whether strange dogs were to be accepted or sent packing. I found these tellings-off a bit confusing, to be honest. Sometimes I'd find myself put on a lead, and then I used to get in a bit of a strop.

Anyway, on the forest walks with Adrian, things were different. For a start, I didn't get let off the lead, ever. I didn't, as it happens, mind this too much. So long as we kept moving forward and I was allowed to stop and check out p-mails (liquid communications used by dogs usually left on lampposts, trees and other prominent locations), I was quite happy. The other big change was that when he saw other dogs approaching, I would often be put in a sit. I was not sure about this – I had things to do, dogs to check out, people to get pats from. Putting me in a sit stopped me, and I did not like this much. That said, while I was sitting, I used to get verbal praise and the odd pat, and I really liked that.

The problem was that if I didn't stay in the sit, I'd find myself in a down position. When that happened, I'd be kept in the down position until I stopped trying to get up. Once I stopped struggling and relaxed, I'd get some praise, a pat on the head and be allowed up again. If I stayed in the sit, then, eventually, I would be allowed to meet the other dogs and humans. The other humans always seemed to be quite impressed with me. Well, they would be, wouldn't they? I had to be careful with other dogs, though. The merest hint of a growl, the merest stiffening of my body, I'd be whisked out of there and I'd find myself lying on my side in what Adrian called, in human-speak, the "relax position".

I also noticed that sometimes we would just walk past the other people and dog. If I tried to cut across to say hello to them, I was blocked. I think it was the more excitable dogs that we ignored. We also ignored any that looked aggressive – he seemed to know which ones these were. Impressive.

The thing is, I really enjoyed the forest walks with Adrian. If I didn't get to meet a dog, it was soon forgotten as we strode forward through the trees. In a way, I didn't have to worry about the other dogs; I could just get on with doing my own thing. That was liberating. Don't get me wrong, I still considered myself to be pack leader, the alpha dog. But in these forest walks, I was happy to let Adrian take the lead, so long as I kept enjoying the walks.

George's Arrival

By now, Nicole and Adrian had moved in together and we all now lived in the country. We had a nice, warm house and a huge garden. I mean huge. It was full of interesting places: there was a small stream on one side, and a pond and an expanse of grass that seemed to go on forever. There was a fence at the far end; I went down there one day to have a look.

There were also big birds living in a big cage. Chickens, I think they're called. I quite like chasing big birds, but I'm going to talk about that later. The best bit was that there were wild areas where I could build a bed. I like to get nestled in amongst long grass and make myself invisible. That's quite easy when you're a small biscuit-coloured dog like me.

One day, I was lying in my dog bed pondering. I couldn't decide whether to stay where I was or to go and lie on the floor. I heard a knock on the door. I have never been one to get that excited by a knock on the door, so I stayed where I was, but I pricked up my ears so I could work out what was happening. Some people had arrived. That was interesting; new people usually meant attention. My teddy bear face was irresistible.

I got up, padded around to investigate and found myself face to face with a huge black and white dog and two strange humans. I wasn't expecting that. I didn't get much time to check this dog out before Nicole had whisked me off my feet and put me in my bed. I was about to get straight back out, but she stopped me with a look. She was learning from Adrian, I stayed where I was. I was fine with that and lay there, watching. The huge black and white dog was brought through and all the humans sat down. I noticed that the big dog was kept on a lead.

I lay in my bed and kept an eye on things. I like my bed, as it happens. It's sort of round with sides and nice and soft. It's just the perfect size for me. I keep my toys there. My favourites are little teddy bears because they're just like me: cute and adorable. I overheard the humans calling the huge black and white dog "George", so I figured that must be his name. I won't say much about him here because he has own section later in the book where he tells his story.

After a while, I was allowed to meet George but, aside from a cursory glance and a quick sniff, he didn't pay much attention to me. I was not sure about that. He was acting as if he was a top dog. Well, two could play at that game. I turned my back and headed back to my bed. Nevertheless, I carried on keeping watch.

The humans stood up, and the two that had come with George departed. It was just me, Nicole, Adrian and George now. George was looking a bit bemused. I guess he was wondering where his humans had gone. George was looking around nervously at, what were for him, his new surroundings. In fact, Nicole and Adrian gave him a guided tour of the house. He was shown where he was allowed to go and where he was not. After that, he was let off his lead. With his new-found freedom, he wandered around the house checking out its scent. It's pretty much what I did when we moved here. George continued to pay little or no attention to me. I mean, he came over and I was just about to get up and greet him, but once again it was a cursory sniff and he was gone. I couldn't quite work out why my heart was beating so fast. I was all aflutter – truth be told, not like me at all.

His inspection complete, he jumped up onto the leather armchair and curled up to go to sleep. I watched with interest. There was a time, before Adrian, that I used to be allowed up onto chairs and sofas, but not anymore. It was my bed or the floor for me. Sure enough, George was turfed out of the chair. In fact, he tried to get on the chair and the sofas a few times. Each time, he was led back to his bed. Talking about his bed, it was huge, a vast spread of comfort covering the floor. It didn't have walls like mine, but it did look inviting. *I'll be having that*, I thought to myself.

In fact, I did try to nick George's bed quite a few times. George never turfed me out. To be honest, he was always pretty gentle with me. My humans were the ones who moved me. I was finding that my "most miffed" expression was not getting me anywhere with them anymore. Anyway, George soon settled in his bed and went to sleep.

Over time, I got to really like George. He was, at heart, a big dog's dog. By that, I mean that he really liked to play with big dogs. He loved the German shepherds next door, and we'd often walk with them. I'd trundle around the field with the humans while George and the two German shepherds tore around playing some pretty powerful rough and tumble. Sometimes, I would get him to play with me too. I'd get up on my back legs and jump up at his side. Sometimes, not always, he'd play and we'd have a little run around. Strangely, for me a terrier, I found myself following George rather than leading him. I think he's the most natural pack leader I've ever met. He had an assertive presence that seemed to fill the room, yet he was as calm a dog as I have ever met. He never lost his temper and was always patient with me.

I was a bit miffed that he ate all my toys, though.

Getting My Way

Author's note: When dogs are stressed or anxious, they can start panting. It's an entirely natural behaviour. Not all dogs do this, but many do. Maxi was such a dog. The problem arises when an anxious dog that is panting gets attention.

When working at DogiPlayce (DogiPlayce is described in detail in George's section), sometimes there would be a thunderstorm or some distant shooting, and this would cause two or three dogs to become anxious. Some charged about, some cowered and some panted. Whatever they did, all the other dogs would ignore them – completely. If we (the dogs and me) were all sheltering from the rain under a tree and one of the anxious dogs was pushing its way through the pack, it was totally ignored. Occasionally, a dog might nudge the anxious dog with its nose. This was an attempt to snap the anxious dog out of it, not to comfort it.

If a human is anxious, it is in our nature to offer comfort. When we transfer this behaviour onto dogs, we are acting as humans, not dogs. The anxious dog interprets the comforting as attention. The anxious dog learns that panting gets attention.

Panting then becomes a method to get attention. This is what happened with Maxi. In her early life, Nicole bought a new bed, but Maxi couldn't get under it. Maxi became anxious, and Nicole did everything she could to comfort Maxi. Maxi learnt that panting got her attention. So, whenever Maxi wanted attention, she panted. If she wasn't getting her way, she panted. The behaviour was reinforced over the years. It became a major issue for Maxi, affecting many areas of her life, and is therefore mentioned a lot in the following chapters.

A dog panting in order to get its way is hard to treat as it is not always practical to ignore the panting dog. In fact, in Maxi's case, while she did stop panting in one or two instances, she didn't really stop till we moved house. In the new house, the triggers that caused her to pant no longer existed, so she just stopped.

Since my rescue in Spain, I had been treated like a princess. This suited me perfectly. When I didn't get my way, I had discovered the best way to change it to my satisfaction was to tremble and pant. By that, I mean that if I didn't get what I wanted, I'd pant or tremble or both until I jolly well did.

It all started many years ago when Nicole changed her bed. One of my favourite sleeping places was under the human bed. In fact, I quite like crawling under things for a lie down. It always feels safe and I can snooze undisturbed. Anyway, I couldn't get under this new bed. I didn't like that and started to worry about where I would sleep. I had nowhere safe to go. When dogs are anxious, we can do a number of things, including panting. The lack of under-bed space had me made me anxious, so I started panting.

This didn't seem to go down too well with Nicole. At first, she didn't do anything, but I could tell she was worried. I could also see that I had her full attention. However, the sleeping arrangements remained unchanged, so I just kept panting. In fact, I panted and trembled and panted and trembled for all I was worth. Nicole started doing all sorts of things to try and distract me. She gave me pats, she played with my toys, she walked me around the flat. She tried many things. However, she didn't get me what I wanted; therefore, I continued to pant. I couldn't speak human, so I couldn't explain the problem to her, so this went on for a long time.

Unfortunately for me, my panting didn't result in my getting the old bed back. But, crucially, I discovered that panting meant lots of attention. I was not aware of it in that instant, but this was a lesson that became etched deep into my subconscious.

In my life since Adrian had appeared there were three things I did not like and wanted to change. One, not being allowed to sleep in the bedroom. Two, being confined to my bed (when I wanted to be somewhere else). And three, travelling in the back of the car (as opposed to on the front seat).

The bedroom issue began after we had moved to Somerset, where I now lived with Nicole, Adrian and George, the huge black and white dog. At first, we all slept in the bedroom. The humans had their bed, and we dogs were not allowed on it. I had learnt that by now and, to be honest, was quite happy with that. I would lie next to the bed on Nicole's side. George had Adrian's side. Sometimes George and I would swap if we felt like it, but, as a rule, it was girls one side and boys the other. The bedroom door was always open, so I could wander off during the night and sleep elsewhere as I pleased. This suited me because I like a bit of privacy from time to time. I could head downstairs and sleep in my bed or even George's huge bed. With the humans asleep, I had George's bed for as long as I wanted. There was no place under the humans' bed but, as I had never been in this house, this did not worry me.

I was glad I was on Nicole's side of the bed because

Adrian used to get up in the night muttering about an awful pong and spluttering and sticking his head out of the window. I could never really figure this out. I mean, I knew George had a tendency to let one or two off during the night, but a smell is just a smell. I had observed that humans, even with their highly restricted sense of smell, sometimes reacted badly to a pong of some sort.

For us dogs, smells are full of information containing detailed information about what caused them. For example, smelling another dog's poo would tell us much about the dog that laid it. George's smells told me much about him. Anyway, I was just glad that I wasn't in danger of being stepped on in the dark. I'm much smaller and probably look like a small rug when stretched out asleep.

It was not long after George moved in that I spied dog beds on the landing. I paid little attention to them. That night, at bedtime, George and I were led to our respective landing beds. George seemed quite happy with this and dozed off. I, on the other hand, ignored the dog bed and trotted back into the bedroom where I lay down to go to sleep. I was hustled out and into my landing bed. That put me in a bit of a mood. I spent much of the night trying to get back in. The humans had left the bedroom door open, so this was not too hard. However, each time I went in, I was spotted and moved back out.

This happened every night. In response, I resorted to the behaviour I had learnt that got me what I wanted – panting. I sat on the landing just outside the bedroom door and panted. And trembled. And panted. And trembled. And panted. It never worked. Once, when I persisted for hours, I found myself locked in a puppy crate downstairs.

Look, I might have given way and changed my behaviour on a few counts by now. I mean, I sat for my dinner. I no longer went charging through the front door the moment it was opened. I sat when I was asked to (most of the time). Lots of things. But I really, really wanted to sleep in the humans' bedroom. I felt it was my right. Finding myself in a puppy crate, I did what any self-respecting terrier would do: I started digging my way out. That made a lot of noise, but it proved difficult as the metal floor was impossible to get through. I was wasting my time – I was stuck there. In the end, I exhausted myself, lay down and went to sleep. In the morning, I was let out as if nothing had happened.

I wasn't about to give up. I'm a terrier; we are tough as old boots and we like to get our way. I persisted for months. Night after night, I panted myself into exhaustion. If not consigned to the puppy crate, I ended up sleeping on the landing floor or in my bed. Or George's bed, for that matter (he liked to stretch out on the floor). Or even Haribo's bed (he joined us a few years after George and had the most comfortable dog bed I had ever seen).

The strange thing is, the day we moved to Scotland this all just stopped. The cycle was broken. If I were to look at this from a human perspective, I'd deduce that having never been in the bedroom in Scotland, I wasn't missing anything. I wasn't trying to get back something I had lost. In fact, in the new house, there were dog beds on the bedroom landing, but we dogs chose to sleep downstairs. In reality, George chose to sleep downstairs because he liked sleeping next to the Aga. Haribo and I just followed George's lead.

Confined to Bed

My second issue was getting confined to my bed. What this meant was that I would be put in my bed and the humans would command me to "stay". I had to stay there till the humans released me. I'd noticed this new "directive" had been creeping into my life over the preceding few months. I was never quite sure why I, the princess, would be confined to bed. But every now and then, I found myself confined to bed.

Needless to say, I was not inclined to obey.

I developed what I thought was a brilliant strategy for dealing with this. By now, I was beginning to learn that direct disobedience just didn't work. If I pushed back against anything the humans asked me to do, I found myself doing what they wanted anyway. It was irritating, but at the same time I had to respect Nicole and Adrian's ability to get me to do their bidding.

Anyway, how did I get out of bed? I could usually see Nicole and Adrian sitting on the sofa or somewhere else close by, so I knew they could see me. I had to be smart. My approach was to leave my bed an inch at a time. I'd start in my bed. After a few minutes, I'd execute what is best described as a "snail manoeuvre". I'd do a small body shuffle that would move me an inch or so. A few minutes later, I'd repeat this. Bit by bit, I'd inch my way across the floor towards my destination.

Sadly, this didn't work. Once I got about a dog's length from my bed, I would be ushered back. Not that this stopped me from trying again. And again. And again. We terriers are nothing if not persistent. The worst time was when Nicole's brother, Matt, was visiting. I might have mentioned it already, but Matt is one of my favourite humans. I love him to bits.

It was after dinner and we'd all eaten. The humans were sitting on the chairs and sofas watching the TV screen. George had gone to bed and was fast asleep. I wanted attention from Matt, so started trying to get it. I tried a number of tricks including the sit stare, the single yelp, the light whine and even jumping up at his leg. I mean, surely I was more interesting than some noisy, flickering screen.

Matt ignored me and continued to watch TV. I gave it all I was worth but, after many fruitless attempts, I ended up confined to my bed.

So, I executed my snail manoeuvres and inched towards

him. As described earlier, I'd get so far before being moved back into my bed. With each block, I got more and more irritated and eventually fell back on that tried and tested approach: panting. I opened my eyes as far as I could, sat in my bed and panted and trembled for all I was worth. Eventually, I ended up in the puppy crate in the kitchen. Even then, I didn't give up. I carried on panting and trembling and even tried a bit of digging. Not for long, though, as by now I had tired myself out. I lay down and went to sleep. A bit later, Matt took George and me out for a walk, and that was great.

It also turned out that Matt was sleeping downstairs on the sofa bed, so I was able to sleep on the floor next to him. That was great, too. That evening, George's naughty streak manifested itself; but that's another story, which I'm sure George will tell you all about later.

Car Journeys

My third issue was car journeys. What you need to know is that my place in a car had always been on the front seat. I don't mean the driver seat, obviously. I'm a dog – I can't drive. I'm talking about the passenger seat. Either I'd have the seat to myself or I'd be on the lap of the human sitting there. I could put my paws on the dashboard and look where we were going. If the window was open, I could hang my head in the breeze.

It had become my right.

This changed after George came to live with us. One day, we headed off on a car journey and I found myself in the back with George. Let me say that again, we were PUT IN THE BACK. I was not happy at all, and believe I sat there with a real strop face on. It hadn't occurred to me that the humans couldn't see this because the back of their seats obscured the view.

I think I've made myself clear. Car journey. Me. Front seat.

Anyway, there we were in the back. George, with his usual grin on his face, looking out of the window watching the world go by. I looked around. There was plenty of room and I could get right up to the back of the front seats. They were, however, too high to get over and the gap too narrow to get around the side. There was a gap in the middle that I thought I might be able to squeeze through. I tried to squeeze through, but was pushed back and found myself back where I had started.

Something you might have noticed, I no longer snarled or growled when I was blocked.

Anyway, the middle gap route was no good; I couldn't get through that way. Next, I tried jumping up against the back of the seat. In the past, I had learnt that this was a good way of getting humans' attention. It didn't work here. I was stuck in the back. As my attempts to get through were thwarted, I got more and more irritated. As I may have said, I had learnt that there was only one thing for it when in a mood.

Panting.

I put my strop face on and panted for all I was worth. You can probably guess what happened. Nothing. The humans just ignored me. Even George ignored me. I probably should have given up, but it wasn't in my nature to give up easily. I just kept panting.

The thing is, when it came to car journeys, panting sometimes worked. This inconsistency didn't sit well in my head. Some journeys I was in the back, and some I was in the front. Note, human and dog logic will see the following situations differently. From the human perspective, I only got to sit in the front because the back was full of stuff. It had nothing to do with panting. From my dog perspective, my panting had got me what I wanted.

The first was a journey in the Land Rover Defender.

Now, the Freelander was bad enough, but in the Defender, the front seats were in a different compartment. Once in the back, there was nothing I could do. On this particular journey, there were three dogs including me. My companions were George and Kika, a dog that was staying with us. We were bundled into the back, the door shut, and off we went.

George and Kika got on really well, so they just lay down, entwined with each other, and went to sleep. I know I could have joined in. I liked George, and I knew he liked me too. He was always pretty tolerant of me and my ways. I got on fine with Kika, too. But I was in a mood. I was not on the front seat and I was miffed. I didn't pant. Even I could see that, with a solid barrier between me and the humans, I'd be wasting my time. But I sat in the corner in a "strop sit" the whole journey. And it was not a short journey. It was about 3-4 hours, I think. But I sat there, in the corner, strop face on full, the whole way. Only, nobody seemed to notice. Or care. So that was a journey where my actions failed to get me what I wanted.

Another journey was the drive to a place called DogiPlayce. We used to go three times a week, and it was only about a five-minute drive. However, I'd get into a strop even for these short journeys. Sometimes I'd even pant. Part of me knew it was pointless, as it was always Adrian driving and he never paid any attention to my strops or my panting. But I couldn't help myself.

If I panted, I'd often find myself left in the car till I stopped. Sometimes I'd stop straight away and be rewarded with a pat and lifted out of the car. Other times I just panted harder. The thing is, I'd be in the car on my own so there was no one to pant at. Once I stopped and relaxed, Adrian would appear and I'd be let out as if nothing had happened.

From a human perspective, this might all sound a bit tiresome. However, from a dog's point of view it makes perfect sense. If the human had let me out while panting, it would have reinforced the panting behaviour. By that, I mean it would have taught me that panting got me what I wanted. The consistent "pant – remain; no pant – let out" message meant that, little by little, the old panting habit was being replaced by a new behaviour: "sit and calmly wait". Old habits die hard; it took months and many journeys.

A third journey was quite different. This was a really long journey, eight or nine hours at least in a big white van. When we set off, I found myself on Nicole's knee in the front seat. I was ecstatic. George was on the middle seat, and Haribo was in the footwell. It was a bit cramped, but it was bliss. Needless to say, there was no panting, trembling or strop sits on that journey.

The final journey I remember was when we moved to Scotland. This was a long journey, too. My humans were in separate cars each pulling a trailer. I was on the front seat in the Defender. I had my place back again. I was a happy wee dog, let me tell you.

To reiterate, in my mind, being able to sit on the front seat again was down to my panting. From the human's perspective, it was simply what was practical on those journeys. We see things so differently sometimes.

The funny thing is, my car journey panting also stopped when we moved to Scotland. I'm not sure why. Perhaps it's because we didn't do as many car journeys. We didn't go to DogiPlayce anymore, so that was three journeys fewer a week. Sometimes we drove for a while and walked in the hills. I used to get in a bit of a strop, but I didn't pant anymore.

Perhaps I had finally learnt that panting was no longer successful in getting attention. Also, I had learnt that there were other ways to get attention, such as lying in my bed looking cute, which worked a lot better.

Packing My Bags

As my story should be making clear, I am a pretty intelligent and independent dog. I like to get my way and while I'm finding this doesn't happen so much these days, I am pretty happy with life. That's not always the case, though. Sometimes things happen which I don't like and all my barked instructions are ignored. Sometimes I give up, but other times I take matters into my own hands.

Long before Adrian appeared on the scene, Nicole would sometimes take me to this place full of other dogs. It was a house and there were quite a few dogs both in the house and in the garden. These dogs also seemed to be visitors, like they were on holiday or something. While we were pretty free to do as we pleased, I did not like being left here.

I made sure Nicole knew this. As soon as we were through the gate, I'd start playing up and barking. When this didn't work and especially when Nicole went back through the gate without me, I'd bark loudly at her. I was telling her to come and get me. She never did.

Every day, all the dogs would be taken for a walk. We'd all be put on our leads and off we'd go. We tended to be taken on the same route every day. We'd walk through the village and along a country path until we reached the woods. There, some of us would be let off our leads and allowed to run around. I was one of those allowed off lead.

For the first couple of days, I'd mooch about, smell some p-mails and leave some p-mails of my own. When called back, I'd obediently trot over. On the third day, I noticed that the human's attention was focused elsewhere. She seemed totally unaware of what I was doing. Opportunity! I headed straight off. I haven't found a fence that can keep me in, yet, and this was true here. I found a gap, squeezed through and took off across a field.

As I made my way, I couldn't help but notice an

interesting smell in the air. It smelt like sausages – burnt sausages, in fact. I changed direction and headed towards the source of the smell. A couple of fences later, I found myself in a street with houses on both sides. Following my nose, I soon located the source of the smell.

There were no gates or barriers, so I was able to trundle right through to the back garden. There were quite a lot of people there and lots of interesting food smells. I put on my best teddy bear face and wandered in. I wandered amongst the humans looking up. It wasn't long before one crouched down and started chatting to me and giving me pats. I looked at her hand, which had food in it, and before long I had a piece of sausage all of my own. Job done.

I scoffed that down and went in search of more. My teddy bear face was working because I got lots of attention, lots of pats and, best of all, lots of sausage. It was great. A bit later, and I don't know how she found me, a lady turned up and took me away. I was unable to repeat this escapade, as I found that I wasn't allowed off the lead again on the dog walks.

This experience had taught me something: if things are not going to my satisfaction, I could just "pack my bags" and head off somewhere else. It opened up all sorts of possibilities of attention and food.

One day, in the country house in Somerset, a visitor came. A human visitor, that is. I remembered her from Spain. I liked her, but I was also suddenly scared. Something had stirred in my subconscious. A human interpretation might have been that I was worried she'd come to take me back to Spain. I don't know; I was just scared all of a sudden. The front door was open, so off I went. As the humans were all busy barking at each other, I was able to leave unseen.

I set off down the garden and across the huge expanse of grass. It was quite a long way before I got to a fence. I looked for a gap but, annoyingly, I couldn't find one. I wasn't sure what to do. I didn't really want to go back, so I lay down and dozed off. A bit later, I was woken by Nicole who had come to get me. I got lots of attention. I had learnt something new. Packing my bags and running away got me great attention.

Thunder and Lightning

At some point during my life, I developed a fear of thunderstorms. It wasn't always this way. When I was young, I wasn't bothered by them at all. Something must have happened along the way. Actually, it's not just thunderstorms; any large bang can set me off. By setting me off, what I mean is I go berserk. I go into a trance, time passes and then I come to. I don't really remember anything, but the room I'm in usually looks different afterwards, as if something has been charging around, bouncing off walls, knocking things over and just creating a huge mess. I suspect that if you were able to witness this, you'd see me panting, trembling, scrambling frantically, drooling, staring and generally just charging around in a panic. When I come to, I am exhausted.

I can detect approaching storms long before my humans, and the smell of one is often enough to set me off. George seems indifferent to thunderstorms. He just lies there watching the world go by. I can remember smelling a thunderstorm coming as we were getting to the end of a walk. I started to bounce around on the end of the lead as if I were on a pogo stick. I was with Adrian and George, and we were by the gate into the sheep paddock. Adrian just sat down, put me on my side (what he calls the "relax position") and waited. I struggled for all I was worth, but to no avail.

Strangely, I remember everything. Perhaps I didn't go into my full trance. George was just lying there chilled out.

The sheep were just the other side of the gate and they were watching me. Adrian seemed to be talking to the sheep. I wriggled and wriggled, but I was held there till the storm passed. We all just sat there listening to the thunder. From a human point of view, it might seem that Adrian was hoping some of the calmness of all the animals would have a calming effect on me. After a while, the thunder passed, I calmed down and we headed back to the house.

Over time, the humans tried many ways to snap me out of these turns. A common approach was to put me in a puppy crate and have George lie down nearby. The puppy crate certainly stopped me bouncing off the walls and knocking everything over. But it didn't improve my mood. I'd just pant and try to dig my way out.

Perhaps it's because this didn't happen very often that I didn't get exposed to all this calm energy emanating from George, the other animals and the humans often enough. Perhaps if it had happened every day, something might have clicked. But, I suppose, even the humans couldn't conjure up thunderstorms on demand.

Another approach was distraction. I confess, this was probably not easy. If I were bouncing around like a demented rabbit, it would have been impossible to get my attention, let alone persuade me to do something else.

However, it did work a couple of times. Once, before we moved to the country, I was round at Adrian's place and a thunderstorm struck. I went straight into my "berserk" mode. Next thing I remember, I was on the end of a lead and running through the snow next to Adrian. I say running, it was more like bounding and leaping because it was quite deep. Quite deep for me, anyway. That was great fun, bounding through the snow. By the time we got back to the house, I was worn out and had completely forgotten about the storm.

Another time we were in a town in a park next to some old abbey or church or something. There were lots of

31

people around and I think there was some sort of human fayre going on somewhere nearby. I think it was even a bit busy for Nicole and Adrian because they had found a bench in a quiet corner where we all paused for a rest. Then, I heard a mammoth *BANG*. I jumped out of my skin and landed in berserk mode.

Next thing I remember, I was on a lead walking along a crowded pavement. I had to get my wits in gear to avoid being stepped on. I could still hear bangs going on, but all my focus was on looking where I was going.

Overall, something had changed. I don't know how it happened, but I noticed my reaction to loud noises was different. Often, after we got back from a walk, we dogs would be given a treat. Now, I had to keep mine away from George in case he nicked it. Not that he ever did; in fact, I don't even remember him trying. But it was my instinct to guard my food. Anyway, I'd found a spot on the grass, next to a tree, and was chewing away. There was a crash of thunder. To be honest, I hadn't even noticed a storm coming. I sniffed the air. Yup, definitely a thunderstorm. I looked up at the sky. I looked down at my chew. I hesitated for a moment, then lay down and carried on chewing my chew.

To be honest, I never completely got over my fear of thunderstorms. But I don't think I ever went berserk again. It's hard to be sure, as my sense of time is different from humans. Nevertheless, we had thunderstorms in Scotland and I don't remember losing it, nor do I remember being in a crate.

Something must have changed.

The Hens

One of the joys in life I think I have mentioned is chasing squirrels. I've never caught one, but it's great fun chasing them. Another joy is chasing large birds like ducks or geese. When we moved to the country, I couldn't help but notice that there were some chickens living in the garden. They had their own patch that was fenced off and was an area that outwitted even my abilities to get in, so I soon lost interest.

However, sometimes they were let out into the wider garden. You'd think I would have taken my chance to chase them, but no, I was tied up. Can you believe it? I was tied to a pole. I was on a long rope but not long enough to get near the chickens. Next to me was a plantation of tall, fern-like plants. Asparagus, I think the humans called it. I amused myself by weaving in and out of these plants till I couldn't move. That usually got a human's attention, and they'd come and free me. Then they'd tie me up again. It was a good game; I kept playing it.

You might be wondering why I didn't put two and two together and realise that I was tied up because the humans knew I'd chase the chickens. Solution: stop chasing chickens. It's because I'm a dog and we can't construct that kind of logic. As a dog, I'm programmed to chase things. It's hardwired into my nature and I can't help it.

One day, something different happened. The hens were in their run and I was running loose in the garden. I was quite happy. All of a sudden, I was scooped up and placed next to the hen run. I say placed, but I was actually put in the "relax position" with my back to the chickens. I wasn't sure what to make of this, but I struggled to lie there while I could sense those chickens close behind me. I wanted to turn around and see what they were doing.

I tried but found that I was not allowed to turn my head. There I lay, pinned to the ground, the chickens right behind me, and I WASN'T EVEN ALLOWED TO LOOK! Can you imagine how this felt? I knew by now that struggling was futile, but I couldn't stop myself. I struggled and wriggled for all I was worth, but to no avail. In the end, I wore myself out. I let out a deep breath and gave up. What did the humans do? They gave me a pat! A pat for lying there and doing nothing. I took advantage and enjoyed the moment.

This went on for days. Every day, I'd be placed in the "relax position" next to the chicken run. The chickens would come over and peck at my fur through the fence. I was blocked when I tried to look. I'd wear myself out wriggling. I'd give up and relax. I'd get a pat. After a while, I found myself accepting this and going straight to giving up and taking the pat.

Things changed again.

I was still tied up when the chickens were out, but now I was tied to a pole in a different part of the garden, next to a patch of grass. I was right in the path of the chickens. Sure enough, when they were let out, they headed in my direction. I waited till they were close and lunged. I didn't get very far because my rope was quite short. The hens didn't move. I found myself back in the asparagus. More days of lying by the chicken run followed. A few days later, I was back tied to the pole in the grass and the chickens were heading my way. It was strange, but I seemed to have lost interest in them. They got so close they were almost touching my nose. Instinct kicked in and I lunged. You've got it. Asparagus. Relax position. Pats. Try again.

I don't know how long this went on; it was a few human weeks. One day, I found myself loose in the garden at the same time the hens were out. I think the nasty wee dogs next door had launched themselves at the fence. The humans had gone to intercept George who was barking at them. In the commotion, I'd been left loose. I couldn't have cared less about those yappy dogs. I wandered off and, in the process, meandered through the chickens. I'd lost interest in the chickens by now. I went over to look at the beehive instead. I like the bees; they let me get right up to the entrance and look in. I've never got stung, ever.

After that, I headed off to crawl under a car and catch some sleep. On the way, I got lots of pats from the humans. They seemed very happy about something. I wasn't sure what that was all about, but I didn't mind. I crawled under the car and went to sleep.

Berry Picking

We went for walks pretty much every day. I liked these walks. Now, it's important for humans to understand how we dogs see our walks. I know there's all this stuff about the pack going for a walk, the pack moving together and so on. That's all very well, but walks are also a chance for us dogs to catch up on what has been going on around us.

We do this by checking on all the smells. We can tell what humans have been where; what animals have done what. Some dogs like to track the movement of cats. George was one of those. I quite liked being social with cats but George, he liked to chase them. Each to our own I suppose. I'm not sure if George had ever seen a squirrel and experienced the joys of chasing one of those.

In order to do these sorts of activities, we need an element of freedom. By that, I mean we need to be able to wander around, stop, read p-mails, sniff scents, backtrack, follow a scent, mark some scents, and so on. The humans can carry on as they please; we can always catch up in our own time. It can be extremely annoying for us dogs when we're kept on a lead and dragged past all those scents waiting to be checked. I think George and I are agreed on this. In fact, sometimes we have to walk right next to the humans. That's kind of bittersweet. I like the moving forward at a constant pace. I like it a lot. But I hate missing out on the sniffing around – something that is instinctive to me. I suppose I could live with all that except, sometimes, the humans themselves keep stopping for various reasons.

A prime example of this is picking berries. There we are, walking along, and all of a sudden we've stopped! I get tied to something and the humans start picking berries. They stop, pick a few berries, look around, move forward a few paces, backtrack, pick more berries, and so on. It seems to take forever.

I really hate stopping. OK, let me clarify that, I hate being forced to stop. If I want to stop and check something out, that's perfectly fine. But I don't like being kept waiting by the humans. Berry picking drives me nuts. I sit there watching the humans. I glare at them. I put my best strop face on. It's all a waste of time; they just don't care. George seems indifferent. He just lolls about or lies down and waits.

Why don't the humans let me off the lead to wander around? There's plenty I could be doing. And if the humans are taking too long, I can always head off back home or go on another sausage hunt. My sulk sit has no effect. I just have to wait till the berry picking is done and we can carry on. I have to admit, this is one area of life where I seem to have no influence on Nicole and Adrian whatsoever. Maybe I should just accept it and lie down like George. But it's not in my nature, as a princess, to do that.

Pausing to pick berries is bad enough, but even worse is stopping midway along a walk for the human to do some random activity such as taking a picture, having a picnic or admiring a plant. These activities can take anything from a few minutes to what seems like an eternity. Sometimes we go out to the field and just stop. I hate that. I've had to sit and watch human activities such as planting trees, burying plastic tubes (pipes) and even chopping up fallen trees. Why am I there? I just don't get it. Every time, I find myself in a sulk sit glaring at the offending human. George, for some reason, is not even on a lead or tied up. Yet, with all that freedom, he just lies down nearby and keeps watch.

Anyway, one day I, too, was left off lead. I was not tied

up. I could wander freely. We were in one of our fields, which was surrounded on all sides by fencing. I lay down for a while and watched things. The human, Adrian, was engaged in some time-consuming human activity. I waited till he wasn't looking and wandered off. I trotted along the path till I came to a fence. There was no obvious way through, so I trotted along by the fence looking for a gap I could either get through or crawl under. Finally, I found one, down near the corner. I squeezed through and trotted off over the grass. This was cut grass, and I could smell humans and a cat that must've lived nearby.

Anyway, I trotted over in the direction of home and found a way out of this grassy area. I crossed the road and found myself at my garden gate. It was closed. What next? I knew. The memory of sausages sprang into my mind. I'd never forgotten my escapade that had led to me getting sausages. This was another such opportunity. I set off up the road. I trotted past where George's German shepherd friends Luna and Bear lived. I suppose I could have popped in there, but the gate was shut. I trotted indifferently past the house where the nasty wee dogs lived, around the corner and into a garden. I thought I'd heard something in there. I couldn't smell sausage, but, well, you never know. I didn't find any sausage, but I did find a nice lady. We made friends straight away. For some reason she examined my collar. Not sure why she did that, or why I mention it, it's not that interesting really. We sat in her garden for a while, and then Nicole appeared. I greeted her, and she took me home.

Grooming

I think I might have mentioned that I'm not too keen on being handled. There was that time when Nicole tried to take my chewy treat off me. Yes, it was stuck in my throat, but I still tried to take her fingers off. That was not the only time I showed my disapproval. I am one of those dogs that doesn't moult. However, my fur keeps growing, so my humans see fit to trim it from time to time. It also grows over my eyes, which is, to be fair, a nuisance as it obstructs my vision. The fur around my mouth can also get pretty dirty, becoming caked up with a mixture of food and dirt.

If you're a human, you'd think I'd be pretty happy for my humans to deal with these problems. Far from it.

In fact, I hated being handled for any reason. Don't get me wrong, I don't mind the odd pat; but when I'm patted, I can walk away if and when I've had enough. What I hate is having my movement restricted. The thing is, as a dog, I didn't know why I was being handled. I didn't know my fur-hampered vision was going to be restored. In the moment, I was being restricted, and I didn't like it. So, it was snarls and snapping teeth all round.

That said, when I was dropped off at a dog grooming salon, things went very differently. I reckon they'd had a lot of experience handling feisty little dogs like me. It was in, wait my turn, on the table and zip, zip, zip – all done before I'd had a chance to react.

At home, it was very different. For a start, Nicole made known her intentions by laying out the tools of the trade. Once I saw those scissors, I was off and hiding in one of my many hiding places. I could defend myself pretty well in one of those. Any hands reaching towards me made an easy target for my sharp little teeth. Sometimes that was enough and the grooming was avoided. I learnt that I could avoid handling by being aggressive.

However, sometimes, Nicole was persistent and waited for me to emerge. The thing is, I'd soon forget why I was hiding and then I'd get bored. I'd wander back into the living room, and Nicole would pounce on me. In fact, it usually took two humans to control me. As a rule, Matt, and later Adrian, would hold me, and Nicole would snip away at the fur around my mouth and eyes. Of course, I'd wriggle and snarl and try to bite them. I'd keep going until they gave up and let me go. I don't think it really registered at the time that I could see better and my mouth felt better too. Nicole never tried to clip me, though, as that was always done by the poodle parlour.

When we moved to the country, Nicole decided she was going to clip me herself. I'd heard talk that she and Adrian had done a sheep shearing course. They probably thought that if they could shear a sheep, they should easily be able to clip a small dog like me. One day, I found myself in the "relax position" for no apparent reason. I was used to this by now, so I didn't really mind. I just lay there and waited to see what would happen next. Then the clipping tools appeared. They were lined up in front of my face and I'd be given my favourite tickle. This happened a few times; I started looking forward to seeing those clipping tools. I couldn't help it.

I got used to this routine, and then it changed. I was lying there, relaxed, when Nicole started to do the clipping. At first, I felt a bit of panic and tried to snap at Adrian. However, I had learnt that, try as I might, I never managed to bite Adrian. Snarling seemed to make no impression on him either. He just ignored me. So, while Adrian held me, I had little choice but to let Nicole get on and trim my fur. It wasn't that bad, really. When it came to my eyes, Adrian held my head in a way so I couldn't move it. I did try but eventually gave up.

The thing is, I found I kind of enjoyed it. Partly it was the attention. I had both humans' full attention, and I liked that. I could sense that George was jealous, and I have to admit that I kind of liked that too. I also learnt to enjoy the sensation of being clipped. Nicole had got hold of proper dog clippers; they were tickly, in a nice way. I was never quite as happy with the snipping around my eyes and mouth, but it wasn't unpleasant either, so I suppose I had

o try and block it. Now, don't get me wrong, I
lapdog and have no desires in that direction, but I
got to like these grooming sessions.

In fact, over time, I just relaxed and let Nicole get on
with it. One day I noticed that I wasn't even being held.
Nicole was doing all the clipping on her own. I suppose I
could have wriggled, snapped and got away but, to be
honest, I felt pretty chilled and just let her get on with it.

In the grand scheme of things, I had one less thing to
worry about, and that was a good thing.

Flystrike

*Author's note: Flystrike is something that most commonly happens
with sheep. It occurs when blowfly lay eggs in the wool, usually in dirty
patches. The eggs hatch and the larvae burrow into the flesh.
Untreated, a sheep will die within a day or two.*

All these changes to my behaviour had made my life feel a
bit different. What I'd noticed was that I was less anxious
than I used to be. To be honest, I was a pretty happy little
dog. Also, I think that the humans and I had a better
understanding of each other. We had a better relationship. I
felt more secure. Don't get me wrong, I was still a princess,
perhaps just a more self-aware kind of princess, if you get
my meaning.

There was one incident that brought this into sharp
focus. We had been at DogiPlayce all morning. I have to
admit, DogiPlayce wasn't really for me. George loved it, but
for me there were just too many dogs. As a rule, I'd find a
quiet spot and sleep till it was time to go home. The other
dogs generally left me alone. Some were like me, some lay
down in the middle of the field, some prowled and some
played. I slept.

On this particular day, I had found a quiet spot under a

hedge in the shady part of the field. It was OK, but there were a lot of green flies buzzing around and landing on me all day. I didn't really pay them that much attention. The next day I could feel something itchy on my skin between my back legs. It was hard to reach and licking it didn't help, so I tried to scratch it by dragging my bottom along the ground. The humans were busy examining a sheep, so I thought they were too busy to notice. However, I was suddenly scooped up and placed in front of a stranger – the vet, as it turned out. She popped my anal glands, which was a bit of a surprise. Released and somewhat indignant, I trotted off before she got the chance to do that again.

The itch was now driving me mad, so I started panting. I found a corner and lay there panting. Normally, this type of behaviour would be ignored, but I was only in the room for a few minutes before I looked up to see Nicole and Adrian looking down at me. I sat there and looked right back. I was in a strop, yes, but not with the humans. They must have seen something because, although I was panting and acting up a bit, they stayed.

After barking gently to each other, Nicole knelt down and gave me an all over body inspection. While I was on my back, she muttered something to Adrian and he disappeared. In the old days I'd have fought back, but with all the grooming experience, I was content to lie there and, well, just relax, basically. Adrian returned with something and handed it to Nicole. Both humans looked a bit worried, but I could tell they were not upset with me. That was a relief. Maybe they could do something about my itch.

I was laid onto a towel, on my back, and Nicole sprayed my itchy area with something. It was cold and I nearly reacted, but I didn't. In fact, moments later, my itch started to ease. Then, Nicole started picking something off my skin. I stretched to have a look. They looked like tiny white worms. There were lots of them, and she picked off every one of them. It was quite a relief and I felt much better.

After a few minutes, my itch was gone and I was back to normal. My humans had understood that my strop was not the usual panting strop, and I had understood that they were trying to help when I was put on my back.

All in all, it turned out well.

On Reflection

I'm getting on a bit in years now, and all in all I reckon I've had a pretty good life. In a way, it has been a life of two parts: before Adrian and with Adrian.

Before Adrian, I was treated a bit like royalty and became something of a princess. I did meet some dog-knowledgeable people along the way and, believe it or not, I was pretty good at off-lead heel walking for a while. But being treated like royalty came at a price, and I developed a few issues along the way. The upside of those is that I used to get a lot of attention when I lost the plot. So not all bad – quite good really.

I have also touched on my fears: thunder, cattle grids and loud bangs. As well as some of my learnt (bad) behaviours: barking at the table and panting when I don't get what I want, to name a couple. I say "bad" behaviours, but this is a human judgement. To me, they were just behaviours I had learnt because I could use them to get what I wanted. Barking at the table got me food. Panting got me attention and usually what I wanted in the first place.

The biggest changes in life with Adrian were twofold. First, my issues were no longer indulged. Second, my "bad" behaviours ceased to work. At first I was pretty aggravated by all this – some things more than others. I mean, not being allowed on top of the humans' bed was annoying, but not that annoying as, truth be told, I was quite happy sleeping elsewhere.

Not getting food at the table was really frustrating, especially as my dinner plate was now only available twice a day for short periods. However, I found myself adjusting to that quite easily. Strange – well, strange to me anyway. It was easier once George arrived, as I could see that we were treated equally. George was also, in a way I find hard to explain, a calming influence on me.

Adrian put in place a number of rules, and I had to keep to them. My attempts to bypass rules were simply blocked. If I pushed it too far, I ended up in a puppy crate. Alternatively, if I followed the rules, I got a lot of positives such as attention, pats and treats.

In a way that I couldn't understand (being a dog), all this change took a lot of pressure off me. For example, take the titbits at table scenario. I could feel my anxiety concerning human dinner time long before it was time. Would I get food, or not? It would start when my food bowl was put down, or even earlier. Should I eat now or should I wait and see what I could get from the humans' table? It could be quite a while, hours even, and all that time I'd be worrying about what I would or wouldn't get. I was anxious a lot of the time. These days, I just eat my dinner and head off for a snooze. No pressure, no worries – quite relaxing really.

Not being allowed to sleep on my humans' bed was fairly easy to cope with, but banishment from the bedroom was a different matter. I tried every trick in the book, played every card I had, but it just didn't work. I was pretty sure Nicole would cave in, but I think I gave it away one night when I was sleeping and then saw Nicole up and about, so I started panting there and then. I think this was when she realised that I was in a strop rather than suffering.

Also, over time, with Adrian, I found my fears easing a bit. I am pretty sure I stopped getting freaked out by driving over cattle grids. I could still get a bit freaked out by storms, but sometimes I had something better to do and just ignored them. I never got any attention if I freaked out, so it was a bit of a waste of energy anyway. Took me a while to get that, though.

All in all, life got a bit easier under Adrian. That may seem odd as he was firm and put rules in place, but the thing is, we dogs like a bit of discipline. In our wild state, we have a pack and it's controlled by the pack leader. We all know our place. Discipline is not punishment; it's just knowing what you have to do and getting on with it. It's also knowing that if you push things, you'll get growled at, or even bitten. It's what we learn as puppies from our mother and the other adult dogs.

It's that desire to get the reward we dogs have which humans tap into when they train us.

Looking back, I don't think I ever fully accepted my loss of status insofar as Adrian toppled me from being pack leader. The arrival of George helped a lot, though, as he was a natural dog pack leader, and I couldn't help but instinctively follow him. Not being pack leader took a lot of pressure off me, much as I hate to admit it.

So, if I were asked, I'd have to say meeting Adrian was a positive experience. I suppose it would be a lot better for us dogs if more of our humans could be bothered to actually learn what makes us tick rather than treating us as surrogate children. There, that's me signing off with something deep and meaningful.

George

George

I'm George, and I am a mix but mainly Anatolian shepherd. I was born in Greece – Athens, to be exact. I am black and white and weigh in at around 45kg. I'm a bit bigger than a German shepherd. I have long legs and look like a wolf when I walk slowly towards you. My breed is native of Turkey, where we are bred as companions for shepherds and guardians of livestock. We are guard dogs and fiercely loyal to our pack. We are independent thinkers, so we can come across as quite stubborn. We do like to know why we are being asked to do something.

Humans think we need careful but firm handling. Basically, if we are to be kept as a pet, I have to confess that our humans need to be pretty expert in handling dogs. This is principally down to our independent nature. We are not easy to train, so it is all too easy to lose control of us. This can lead to potentially dangerous situations; for example, people and other dogs can be easily scared by our size, looks and boisterous nature. We can also get ourselves into danger if, for example, we take a dislike to cars or trains and chase them.

When guarding livestock, our main approach is to bark warnings at any intruder and hope that's enough to scare them away. Boy, do we love to bark. If that doesn't work, then we'll pile in, full-on assault mode, and send the intruder packing. We are bigger than wolves, which is important as they are the main threat we have to deal with.

My first memory is being in a cardboard box with my brother. We were tiny wee puppies. We could hear noises, like cars going by, and we could sense big metal birds in the sky. We were in that box a long time, getting hot, hungry and thirsty. We were starting to panic a little, lose hope even, when all of a sudden we saw this male human peering down at us. We were pretty desperate by then, so we gazed up with the cutest expressions we could muster. It's the only way we thought we'd get out of the box.

It worked. This male human took us into his care. He spoke a different human tongue to what we were used to. Not that it mattered; neither my brother nor I could understand a word of human. No dog can. I sometimes wonder why humans keep babbling on at us. We never understand a word. We just wag our tails and hope for the best. Mind you, we do understand tone. We know when humans are happy, and we know when they are not. I digress.

Anyway, this human sent us on a long journey to a place called England. I tell you what, it's freezing there. Not that I should be complaining; we are supposed to be hardy enough to live rough in the mountains of Turkey. But even so, after the balmy climate of Greece, it was a bit of a shock. I found myself in a tiny house somewhere with a couple of humans and some spaniels. I'll be honest, it didn't work. The humans thought they were dog experts, but breeding a few spaniels had not prepared them for a dog like me.

Imagine a tornado in full force in your living room. That's me – boundless energy, strong, huge, barking at everything that moves and very keen to get my own way. I was not there long and, to cut a long story short, I soon found myself in a fabulous place full of dogs. It was amazing – two fields, a tired old house, some outbuildings and a caravan. There must have been about 50 dogs there, and we all operated as one huge pack. The fields were ours. Our pet human tried to keep some semblance of order but, let me tell you, mealtimes were chaos. We were fed one at a time in a small shed. Whenever the door opened so the next dog could be admitted, we all tried to pile in at once. It was great; I loved every minute.

To be honest, with all that space to run around and big dogs to play with, I think I went a bit feral. I probably got back to my wolf ancestry. It was dog heaven.

Every now and then, I'd be bundled into a van and taken to a human house somewhere. These houses always seemed pretty small. My pet human would look around, say something to the resident humans, then bundle me back into the van and take me back. I used to enjoy these trips; it was something to do. One day, two of my pet humans bundled me into the van and off we went, as usual. I was pretty excited. To be honest, I was always pretty excited. I just liked to have things happening. Living in the moment, I never wondered where we were going.

We stopped at another human house. It was quite small, like the others, but it did have a big garden. Huge, in fact – bigger than the fields in our rescue centre. I also recognised the resident humans. I'd noticed them once or twice at the rescue centre looking at me and sometimes saying, "George." I had been too busy charging around with some of the other dogs to pay them much attention, so I'd pretty much ignored them.

Anyway, I was sitting in this human house, on a lead, waiting for something to happen. It was then that I realised my pet humans and their van had gone and left me here.

First Contact

There I sat in this strange room in this strange place. I wasn't quite sure what to make of things; we dogs like to know where we are. I might be a big dog but, like many dogs, I can get anxious when new or unexpected things happen. New places and new humans all added up to a new pack. I lay down and waited. I wondered what was going on at home – probably chaos as usual. Boy, I loved that place.

I was still on a lead. After a short while, the male human started to walk me around the house. As I was on the lead, I had no choice but to follow. That said, I enjoyed looking around and smelling the new smells. The male human seemed pretty calm and relaxed, and that helped me feel less anxious. While calm, he was also assertive; he seemed to know what he wanted. I liked that about him – those are the qualities we look for in our pack leaders. I like to think I am calm and assertive myself. Maybe I would find myself leading this pack in time.

We trundled around and I was shown lots of what humans call "rooms". The human took me into most of these and let me sniff around. There were a couple where he stood in the doorway and blocked me. I think he was trying to talk "dog" and tell me that those particular rooms were his so I was not allowed in. I filed that information away and never did enter those rooms.

I was starting to relax a little; the humans here seemed calm, and I liked that. We dogs, we don't like nervous energy as it can, in turn, make us nervous. Some of my doggie friends back at the rescue centre, well, they could turn aggressive if the energy turned bad. It's how some of us dogs are wired.

By now, we were back where we had started the tour. The male human took the lead off me, and I was free to wander around. The first thing that caught my attention was the smell of another dog. I looked around and there was a small, biscuit-coloured, fluffy-looking dog staring right back at me. It was a female; I could tell from her smell. She had huge eyes – I think that maybe she was making them look big and round. *Terrier*, I thought to myself. *I might have to keep an eye on her.* The terriers back at the rescue centre could be quite prickly.

I felt the human's hand on my neck. I could tell without looking that it was the female human. Aside from her smell, she was making funny little noises. She was pointing to a big, soft-looking area on the floor. She gently eased me towards it. I sat down on it, and she gave me pats. I liked her straight away. She seemed a bit more excitable then the male human, but that was OK.

After all this excitement, I was starting to feel pretty tired. I looked around and saw a vision for any dog's eyes. In the corner, there was a beautiful leather chair, and it looked to be just my size. We had sofas in my old home, but nothing like this. I got up, wandered over, jumped up onto this wonderful chair and curled up to go to sleep. Bliss!

However, within seconds, I felt the male human's hand on my collar. He was leading me off. I was perplexed. I waited till he let go of my collar and jumped back up again. This was my chair now. But then he did it again, and this time he sat on the chair himself. I studied him, and his body language was quite clear: he was telling me that it was his chair.

OK, I thought myself, *new pack, new territory. I'll back down this time.* I looked around and saw a sofa. We had free use of the sofas at the rescue centre, so I jumped up on this. I made myself comfortable and shut my eyes. I was not there for long. Within moments, the male human's hand was on my collar. He gently, but firmly, led me off the sofa. I looked over at the little dog. She was watching me with interest. She gave nothing away, but I had the feeling she wanted to see how this would play out. I think she was sussing me out.

The male human led me over to the soft space on the floor and got me to lie down. *Right*, I thought to myself, *chair is not OK, sofa is not OK, but soft area on the floor is OK.*

I'll be honest, I was not used to this kind of discipline, especially from humans. That said, part of me was glad of it. We dogs like to have discipline in the pack. For us, discipline simply means rules that we follow. If we step out of line, a higher-status dog or even the pack leader might tell us off. But we all know the rules, and we tend to keep to them. It helps us feel secure. It was only a very short period of time, but already I felt fairly relaxed here.

I was exhausted and the next thing, I was fast asleep.

A little later, the female human woke me. I sprang up in excitement; something was happening. Both humans, the terrier and I went outside. We had a quick tour of the garden and I left a couple of markers. When we went back in, instead of taking me to my bed, the female human led me up the stairs into a room. I could tell from the smell that the humans slept here. There was a big, flat, soft, raised platform that I looked at. The humans called it a "bed". However, following my experience with the chair and the sofa, I waited. I also noticed that the humans had placed something soft on the floor next to this platform.

Anyway, I think the idea was for me to sleep here. The little biscuit-coloured dog was the other side of the bed. Ah, I see, humans on the big bed, we dogs on the floor next to them. That was fine with me, so I lay down and was fast asleep in an instant. Next morning, I was taken outside by the two humans. That was handy, I was able to relieve myself and also set down some more markers. I had to let other dogs know I was here and that this was my territory. I had a good sniff around. I could smell other dogs in various directions. I could also smell some large birds nearby. I couldn't explore too far because I was on a lead and, besides, it wasn't long before we were back indoors.

The humans put me and the little terrier side by side and said that funny word again, which sounds like "sit". I remembered it from the previous evening; they wanted me to put my bottom on the floor. To be honest, I couldn't see the point, so I just stood there and waited. Well, it was in my nature to be independent and think for myself.

That said, I thought terriers were also an independent breed that made up their own minds, but the little terrier had parked her bottom on the floor. The humans said "sit" again and this time, I noticed a treat in front of my nose. As I went to get it, the hand moved up, followed by my nose and before I knew it, my bottom was parked on the floor. I was a bit surprised, but I took the treat.

Next, bowls of food were placed on the floor in front of us. I got up to eat. The humans took the bowl away! I stopped and looked up, as I wasn't sure what was happening. I heard one of the humans saying "sit" again. They were putting food in front of me but telling me to sit. It didn't make sense.

I was puzzled. Had the humans started eating before me, I would have understood it – pack leaders eat first. But sitting for dinner, I hadn't come across this before. I stood and waited. After a couple more times hearing the humans say "sit", I sat and waited. They put the bowl of food in front of me again. I sat and waited. They made another noise, which sounded like "OK" or something. At this point, the terrier got up and headed for the bowl in front of me. The male human moved and diverted her to the other bowl. He then led me to my bowl.

It was a delicious meal. I ate it slowly (I'm a careful eater) and went and lay on the floor to see what would happen next.

Through the Hedge

Author's note: We humans tend to be pretty strict about our boundaries. We mark them with fences, hedges, walls, and so on. To a dog, these boundary markers are irrelevant. A dog will set its own boundaries based on its own perception of who and what lives where. To a dog, fences, hedges and walls are simply part of the general outside. For example, George perceives his domain to include our land, two neighbouring gardens and half the hillside opposite (which is part of another farm).

It is common for dog territories to overlap, which can lead to aggression. An example of this is when a dog barks at you as you walk past its garden. Here, the pavement is also included in the dog's mind as part of its territory, so, perceiving you as a potential threat, it needs to see you off.

It was a sunny day and we were all out together in the garden. By "we", I mean the small terrier (who by now I had learnt was called Maxi), the two humans and myself. My humans were called Adrian and Nicole. I was bursting with energy and ready for a good rough and tumble session with some big dogs. I suppose I could have played with Maxi; she seemed up for it. But, to be honest, I preferred big dogs. I liked to be able to career into them at full speed. Maxi was just too small.

I was not on a lead, so I took the opportunity to have a good look around.

There was a high wall on one side of the garden – too tall for me to jump over. Further down it turned into a fence. That was not too high, and I reckoned I could get over that without much difficulty. However, I picked up a scent that told me other dogs lived there. Two dogs, to be exact, little dogs – terriers, it smelt like. Their scent also told me that they were not balanced dogs. Not being there, they were of little interest to me in that moment.

Further down, on the other side, there was a long hedge with a fence in it. That, like the wall, was too tall for me to get over. However, there was a big wooden gate, and that was definitely jumpable. Beyond that was a road; it smelt like many humans and dogs passed that way. If this was my new territory, then I'd have to keep an eye out here too. If any predators got too close, I'd have to see them off. I looked forward to that, as it was my main purpose in life.

Further back towards the house, there was a small muddy ditch and behind that, a wooden fence. I could smell dogs over there too. Five or so including Labradors. They're more my size, so I looked to see if I could get to them. However, the fence was too high. I gave up and carried on exploring. Next to the house stretched a tall hedge. It was so tall I couldn't even see the top. In front of this was a hen run in which were hens. I could feel Nicole's and Adrian's eyes watching me, waiting to see what I would do. I looked at the hens and knew I'd be looking out for them. To me they were just like sheep; they were part of my flock and so were to be protected.

Anyway, this tall hedge was of more interest to me. Not the hedge itself, but the smell from those who lived behind it. Two German shepherds – a male and a female. The female was the pack leader. Perfect – two big dogs to play with. I wandered over to the hedge and examined it. It wasn't long before I found a gap and went through. It never occurred to me that anyone might object to this.

There they were, waiting for me. They looked a bit aggressive, but before they had a chance to react, I went straight into play mode and careered into the female. In an instant, we were charging around the garden. It wasn't that big, but it was big enough. It was brilliant, just like my old home. Suddenly, an elderly male human came out and barked something, but we just ignored him.

However, it wasn't long before Nicole and Adrian appeared and grabbed me. I was perplexed. Why were they stopping me? I was having a great time. I was pretty sure the two German shepherds were enjoying themselves, too. My humans spoke to the elderly human. It all seemed fine, but, before I knew it, I was led back to my garden.

I have to admit that I was a bit put out by this. However, as I may have mentioned, it is in the nature of my breed to make up our own minds, so I decided to go straight back through the hedge. Again, Nicole and Adrian came and led me back. We repeated this cycle a few times. Then Adrian tied my lead to a tall pole. I was tied up. I was not impressed and made my feelings clear. Nicole and Adrian just ignored me. After a while, I gave up and lay down.

While I lay there, Nicole installed some wire netting along the hedge. I lay there and watched and waited. In time, I was released. I spent a few minutes pondering what to do next before making my decision. I went up to the hedge and walked along the wire netting looking for gaps. Just after the hedge turned up along a ditch, I found another gap. As you can probably guess, it was not long before I was back and tied up again. I didn't really understand the problem. Why couldn't I play with these dogs?

In time, I was released and I headed back to the hedge again. I was determined to get through whatever my humans wanted. I noticed a new post near the corner of the hedge. As I approached it, Adrian issued a warning bark. I stopped and looked around. Sure enough, he was looking right at me. I looked at him, then at the hedge, then back at Adrian. What was the warning for? I wasn't sure. I took another step. Adrian barked another warning. I stopped, then retreated a couple of steps. Adrian made happy noises.

I tried to work this out. I got a warning if I went past the post, so that meant he didn't want me to go past it. I thought about this for a few moments, then decided that I didn't need to obey Adrian, so I walked past the post. Adrian came over, grabbed my collar and I found myself tied to the post again.

We repeated this dance a number of times over the course of the day. It dawned on me that the lesson here was if I got caught passing the post, I'd be tied up. I didn't like being tied up. However, I really wanted to play with the German shepherds. I waited till Adrian was not looking.

However, Adrian was a wily one. He had anticipated my intentions and caught me. At that point, I decided to leave trying to get through the hedge, for now. I'd got the message and had to respect that. In this instance, Adrian was one step ahead of me. I have to confess, nonetheless, that there were a couple more transgressions. However, as a rule, I did as Nicole and Adrian wanted and stayed this side of the hedge.

As it happens, I did get to meet the two German

shepherds most days. We were all taken to a large field and on these occasions, we were allowed to play until we were exhausted. I loved those sessions. I also realised that Adrian was a bit more dog savvy (for a human) than I was used to. Nicole, she was quite dog savvy, but I still reckoned I'd get her eating out of my hand. But I was settling in here, and it was good to have humans that were more dog-like in their behaviour. It helped me to feel secure.

Luna and Bear

The two German shepherds next door were called Luna and Bear. You could often hear their pet male human yelling "Luna" or "Bear", but they tended to ignore him. I reckoned Luna was pack leader in that house, although the elderly female human seemed pretty strong, too.

Anyway, each day one of my humans took me out for walks. I loved these walks and got to know the different routes we took. Best of all was when we went through our gate and turned right. That way lay the village and a special field. We might be heading up to the shop but I know that, if we turned right again, we'd be heading towards Luna and Bear.

The walks involved myself, my human and Maxi, the little terrier. For Maxi, the human's pace was probably quite quick. But for me, it was pretty slow. All I wanted to do was get to Luna and Bear's place as quickly as possible. But my human always made me walk next to their legs. They kept saying something that sounded like "heel". It was just so frustrating. Sometimes, a little squeak of frustration escaped my mouth – I just couldn't help it.

I have to say that Adrian was much stricter. If I pulled ahead, he would just stop and wait for me to back up. That was so hard, having to go backwards when ahead lay fun and games. It was particularly difficult when we walked past

Luna and Bear's garden. It was even harder when they were there because they would come running over to the gate to greet me. But Adrian didn't even seem to notice them; he just kept going, keeping me by his legs. No amount of prancing around, stopping, tugging or whining made the slightest difference.

Still, while I was desperate to go over to Luna and Bear, I also knew that ahead lay the special field I mentioned earlier. So, it was only a few moments before I forgot about Luna and Bear and focused on getting to the field. It was not far – it only took a few minutes to get there. Once there, the human needed to open a gate to let us in. Beyond was a huge expanse of grass.

It was a bit frustrating getting through the gate. My human made us sit while he opened it. We would then have to walk through and sit on the other side while he closed it. I learnt that it was best to do this; otherwise, the human just repeated the process until we got it right.

Once we were through the gate, I then had to sit and wait for the human to take my lead off. That done, the big question was whether Luna and Bear were already there. I already knew because, if they had got there first, I could smell their trail through the gate. My human always took a moment to look around. Could he not smell them?

What I liked best were the times when Luna and Bear had got there first. They would wait with their human about 100m into the field. It was even better when they didn't see me arrive. Either way, as soon as I was released from my "sit" by my human, I would thunder towards them. If they saw me coming, they would race towards me and we'd all collide with an almighty thump. It was great. If they didn't see me coming, I would charge right into one of them, usually Bear, and send him rolling over.

If they were not already in the field, we would walk down the field a way, then we'd turn around to face the gate, stop and I'd find myself in a sit. Again. The human and I watched the gate intently. Maxi never seemed that interested; she just seemed a bit miffed that we were not moving. Anyway, we got to watch Luna, Bear and their male human come through the gate. Luna and Bear never sat for the gate. You could hear their human yelling "SIT!" but they paid him no attention. In fact, their human would bark "SIT!" at them constantly while he was opening the gate. As soon as it was open, they just piled through. Then my human would release me, causing us dogs to charge towards each other.

It was amazing fun. We would charge around chasing each other playing dog games until we needed to stop and catch our breath. Then, we were off again. While we were playing, the two humans and Maxi would wander around the field. We had plenty of time to wear ourselves out. Luna, Bear and I loved these play sessions. Apparently, Maxi and I were the only dogs they ever got to meet, let alone to play with. It seemed many dogs and their humans were scared of Luna and Bear. I never understood why.

I had occasionally been aware of clashes next door. I think the terriers used to crawl under Luna's gate and into their garden. Of course, Luna and Bear being a guard breed would try to see them off. Terriers being terriers, they stood their ground. Even though it was the terriers that caused the problem, it was the German shepherds who got the blame. Usual story, it's always the big dog's fault, even when it isn't.

These were the same unbalanced terriers I had smelt when I first arrived. They had smelt of trouble, and I had been right.

Luna also told me that their human was really pleased that I got to play with them. Apparently, all of us walking back after playtime together and, as the humans put it, under control made him feel really happy. It was his chance to show that his dogs were not as bad as their reputation. I'll be honest, most of this went over my head. I was still really just a puppy; I was only one year old. All I knew was that Luna and Bear were great.

Over time, Luna, Bear and I became best friends. We got to play together most days, which was just great. It was a bit like where I used to live – lots of rough and tumble. I slept pretty well those days.

I also have to admit that I was finding myself respecting the humans more than I had in the past. Adrian, particularly, seemed to understand the ways of dogs. I found myself acquiescing to him rather than trying to lead him. This was a strange experience for me – I was used to leading. Even though I was young, I had led the pack in all my previous homes. It's not that I took charge; the other dogs just seemed to follow me. I was not even sure what I was doing. Maybe it's just my nature. I even think that Maxi, who behaved as though she liked to be in charge, looked up to me.

I was settling in well here – plenty of exercise, a bit of discipline and lots affection, especially from Nicole. Don't get me wrong, I retained my independence as much as I could insofar as I obeyed Nicole and Adrian when it suited me. Mostly, I got away with this – though, not always, as you will find out if you carry on reading.

Greetings

I didn't get to play with Luna and Bear every day. On those other days, we used to go for walks elsewhere. Sometimes, either Adrian or Nicole would take us. Sometimes they both came. There were lots of different routes they took, all rich in smells waiting to be checked. We could find ourselves walking around the edge of fields, along country lanes and through woodlands. Sometimes I was on a lead. Sometimes I was allowed to run free.

I was starting to get the hang of this whole heel-walking

business, but I did forget to do it quite often. Adrian was very strict about this. Nicole, less so. I could get ahead of her from time to time. Sometimes, on these walks, we'd spot other humans and they sometimes had dogs. I loved meeting new dogs. I loved meeting new humans, too, but new dogs even more so, especially big dogs because then there was a chance of a good play.

At first, I would run gleefully towards them ready to give my best greeting. This usually involved me careering into either the new dog, its human (or humans) or all of them, much as I did with Luna and Bear. I have to be honest, I didn't always get the reaction I was expecting. Some of the dogs, especially the smaller ones, would try to bite me. I never reacted. I would just back up a bit and try to say hello again. Sometimes the humans barked at me – not very nice barks either. That could make me a bit anxious. I could get a bit puzzled; after all, I was only trying to be friendly.

I remember that once I tried to charge over to a new human while I was on the lead. I pulled Adrian over, and he clattered to the ground. As a human, Adrian should have known of my exuberant nature, my love of meeting new humans and my propensity to lunge forwards. However, he didn't let go of the lead, so down he went. That pulled me up abruptly, and I looked around to see what was stopping me. Next thing, I found myself in a sit and not allowed to approach the new human.

Anyway, things changed. Adrian and Nicole started blocking me from rushing to say hello. The way they did this was to call me over whenever they saw humans in the distance. We did a lot of what I think the humans call recall training. Adrian seemed particularly keen on this. We'd go into a field and I'd be allowed to wander around. Then, Adrian or Nicole would call my name and make a human bark that sounded like "come". Their arms would be wide apart and they'd have a treat in their hand. I'd bound over and sit, get the treat and a pat too. I liked the pats more than the treats if I'm honest. We did this a lot. In fact, we also did this on walks, which could be a bit annoying. The humans didn't seem to understand that there were more important, or more exciting, things than treats. Also, as an independent breed, surely it was up to me to choose whether I needed to go over to them or not.

Sometimes, the humans would attach a long piece of rope to my collar. If I didn't go over when called, they'd just reel me in. I was learning that they wanted me to go back when called, whatever I might be doing. While I understood this, my independent nature meant that I didn't always want to go back. This, combined with my natural propensity to want to lead the pack, meant that I would, on occasion, see no reason to obey. So, no matter how often we went through this, there was always a chance I'd ignore a recall command.

Anyway, back to the walks. Now, when approaching strangers were spotted, they'd use this recall command to try and call me over. What happened next would depend on where we all were. If Adrian and Nicole were between me and the strangers, I would have to get past them to reach the strangers. On those occasions, I'd obey the recall. If I was closer to the strangers, I had a choice. I could go back, as Adrian and Nicole wanted, or I could rush over and greet the strangers. It was never an easy choice. I'd assess things and then decide whether to obey the recall, or not. I was more likely to disobey if the strangers had a dog with them.

It didn't always pan out as I might have hoped. If I ignored my Adrian and Nicole, they would come and get me and put me on a lead. I'd then have to sit while they chatted with the strangers. I was locked down tight. This was a conundrum for me. We dogs, as a rule, are not too good on cause and effect. I mean, we know how to develop behaviours we can use to get what we want from our humans: treats, pats and so on. But working out that I'd miss out on attention and maybe even a bit of play if I didn't go back when called, that was a bit of a stretch for a dog. So, I would sit there but at the same time be desperate to break free.

Sometimes I would even have to sit close to the new humans and dog, but I wasn't allowed to greet them. I found this very frustrating. I tried many doggy tricks to get around this. For example, whining as hard as I could, but I was just ignored. Sometimes I would try getting up and going over anyway, but I always had a lead attached, and Adrian or Nicole would pull me back and return me to my sit. I also tried all sorts of shuffling, to no avail.

Nothing worked. Sometimes I just gave up and relaxed. Strangely, I would often get a pat when that happened. I even sometimes got a pat from the stranger. Sometimes I'd even be let off the lead again. It seemed that humans liked me to relax – if I did, I was more likely to get what I wanted.

What I did notice was that my freedom was more restricted on these walks. Adrian and Nicole tended to keep me close by. It became almost impossible for me to greet new humans without going through the whole sit and wait process. Over time, I accepted this, up to a point.

Rucksack Walks

We went out for plenty of walks, including a morning walk, a daytime walk and an evening walk. The daytime walk was often quite long. I loved those walks. My housemate, Maxi, trotted along happily. While those walks might have been quite tiring for her and her little legs, for me, I still had plenty of energy when we got back. I'd always be looking for things to do. Of course, top of the list was getting through the hedge. I had, nevertheless, learnt to be very careful about this. I could only try if both Adrian's and

Nicole's attention were elsewhere. If they saw me try, I would be intercepted and tied up. I hated that. I did, however, get through a few times. Each time I was led back to my garden by Luna's human.

And there was always my enthusiasm to meet new people. Adrian worked hard to keep me in check, but sometimes I was just too fast. I couldn't help it; I was only a year old and full of energy. I loved Adrian and Nicole by now, and I wanted to please them, really, but I wanted to play even more.

One day, on getting ready for a walk, Adrian and Nicole put some sort of contraption on my back secured by a strap under my stomach to keep it stable. It was quite heavy, not too heavy, but I was aware of it. I think, from the smell, it had rocks and padding in it. It looked like they were giving me a load to carry.

Off we went. While this load was more padding than rock and therefore quite comfortable, I wasn't that keen as it slowed me down a bit and bounced around if I ran. Nevertheless, I still enjoyed my walk. I was allowed off lead in places and was able to check out all the interesting smells. I found it was harder to rush over and greet new humans and dogs with the same exuberance while wearing this pack. Strangely, it became easier just to do as I was told and wait patiently. There was not much I could do about this pack (I couldn't shake it off), so I just accepted it and carried on.

Something I did notice was that new humans and dogs seemed to be friendlier towards me now. Sometimes when I had rushed over all friendly and excited, I was bitten or barked at. If I waited alongside Adrian or Nicole, I tended to get more attention, and sometimes they would remove my pack and let me off my lead so I could play with another dog.

Over time, I found my behaviour changing. It wasn't that I was getting older and wiser – I still had the same youthful, exuberant enthusiasm for everything that I've always had – I just found that I was more inclined to follow Adrian and Nicole. I suspect this was because wearing the pack meant that I did the "new walk" approach every day on every walk, and it just kind of became the way to do things.

I had been carrying the pack for what seemed like forever, but it was probably no more than a few human weeks. Then, one day, we headed off for a walk with no pack on my back. I was happy to just be me again. Strangely, I found that my new, less exuberant behaviour stayed with me.

We had an interesting experience on one of these walks. Adrian, Maxi and I were walking along a track. It was kind of like a road. We had just passed a farmhouse. We'd been here before and I liked this route. Adrian suddenly stopped and made Maxi and me lie down. At first, I wasn't sure why and was a bit hesitant to obey. It was a bit of a random place to stop, even for a human. Anyway, after a short pause, I lay down as instructed.

Then I heard it – a big dog approaching. My ears pricked up. A few seconds later, a German shepherd appeared looking aggressive. It had run all the way up the hill and through two fields to get to us. I looked at it with interest, but its aggressive nature made me hesitate.

The thing is, it came charging up to us and then stopped a few yards away. Adrian just ignored it and told us we were being "good dogs". I liked that phrase "good dogs". It was always delivered in a tone that I liked. I took my lead from Adrian and did nothing. With Adrian keeping the energy calm, Maxi and I also remained calm, albeit curious. I noticed Adrian's body language: he was standing tall and proud but not facing the German shepherd directly and not looking at it. He was basically telling it, in dog, that he was an alpha dog who was prepared to stand his ground but didn't want to fight. Further, because we were all relaxed, we were also telling this German shepherd, in dog, that we posed no threat.

The German shepherd didn't know what to do and just sat down and looked at us. After a short time, it got up and wandered back to where it had come from.

Ploughed Fields

Reading this, it might seem to you that, by now, I was becoming the perfect, obedient dog. Far from it. I had learnt that in certain situations, it was better to follow Adrian and Nicole's instructions, but in certain situations only. I was still young and full of play, and sometimes I just couldn't help myself.

As I might have mentioned, Adrian and Nicole spent a lot of time trying to teach me to come back when they called. I say trying to teach me, but what I mean is that I'd worked out pretty quickly what they wanted. It's just that I didn't always choose to return when they called. I felt that this was my prerogative as, having been bred to be independent and make my own decisions, it was my choice whether to obey my humans or not. Basically, if Adrian or Nicole called, I'd return to them, unless I had something better to do. Such things included exploring an interesting scent (small furry creatures figured highly), playing with another dog or when I was lying down and couldn't be bothered to get up.

But Adrian and Nicole were a bit more astute than I had given them credit for.

Near our house, there was a large field we sometimes went through. We always walked around the edge of this field. That was fine; there was quite a wide, grassy area for us to walk on. The rest of the field had some prickly, sort of stubbly stuff all over it, which made it a little uninviting. On the odd occasion when I wanted to go there, Adrian and Nicole always stopped me. Mostly, they kept me on a long lead, so I didn't have much choice. Sometimes, they'd let me off the lead, but I kept to the grassy area as it was more interesting.

One day, we went into this field and it had changed. All the stubbly stuff had gone and in its place was a wide expanse of smooth soil. It looked very inviting, and I wanted to run around it as fast as I could. I looked at it longingly, but I was on a lead so there was not much I could do. We walked around near to where we would exit this field. That was through a hedge and something called a stile. The humans would hop over the top of this, and Maxi and I had a gap we could squeeze through.

Anyway, Adrian and Nicole stopped at the hedge and said something to each other. I was in a sit waiting to see what was coming next. What came next was that they let me off the lead. Well, I was off like a shot, straight onto all this fresh soil. Adrian and Nicole called me. Recall? Now? In their dreams. This new soil area was way too exciting. In an instant, I was in full play mode. I ran around in circles, flat out, changing direction, zigzagging, charging this way, then that way.

It. Was. Amazing.

Back on the grassy strip, Adrian and Nicole were stood there calling me. Needless to say, I ignored them. In fact, as soon as they looked at me, I dropped my front legs and presented them with the play bow – a dog's invitation to play. The moment they moved, I was off, running in circles and charging around like a mad thing.

It. Was. Amazing.

Adrian and Nicole called me a few times; each time I adopted the play bow. Again, the slightest movement from Adrian or Nicole and I was off. Part of me was aware that neither Adrian nor Nicole were joining in, and this puzzled me. In fact, I really hoped they would chase me and try to catch me. In that game, I would let them get really close and then just as they reached for my collar, I would zoom off, run around in circles, then stop and readopt the play bow. That would be a great game.

Adrian and Nicole didn't try to catch me. In fact, what they actually did was turn their backs on me. They just ignored me. I wasn't entirely sure what to make of this, so I stopped and observed them. They were looking at something in the distance and barking away to each other in human. I crept up behind waiting for them to turn. As soon as they moved, I'd be off again. But they never looked. They never turned around. In fact, they started to move away. Instinctively, I felt compelled to follow. As I was still young, I still felt like a puppy – and the puppy has to follow the adults. I moved closer until I had caught up with them. I looked up to see if I could work out what was going on. I was wearing my best inquisitive puppy face. Adrian calmly leant over, put on my lead and off we went.

One moment I am charging around having a great time. Then, in an instant – no fuss, no barking, nothing – I'm on the lead and walking alongside them as if nothing had happened. I suspect a small part of me learnt, perhaps, that charging around doing play bows might not be the best approach to get Adrian and Nicole to play with me.

I didn't bother trying that again.

Town Walks

As I think I've said, most of our walks were out in the country or play sessions with Luna and Bear. However, sometimes, we'd be bundled into the car and taken somewhere different. I quite enjoyed the car journeys. I could look out of the window and watch everything go past. Sometimes I'd see dogs in other cars. Some of them used to bark at me, but I just ignored them. There was also plenty of space in our vehicle, so I could lie down and have a snooze if I felt like it.

Sometimes we'd end up in a place with lots of buildings and people. Humans call these towns. This one was called Glastonbury. On arrival, we'd be in a large area with hard ground and lots of cars. Adrian would open the boot. By now, we had learnt that opening the boot was not an invitation for us to jump out. We had to wait. In fact, we had to sit and wait. Adrian and Nicole would use this time to put leads on us. It was a bit like the front door of our house – I wasn't allowed to charge out of that either. I'd tried a few times, but Adrian and Nicole had always either blocked me or taken me back in if I'd got past them.

Once Adrian and Nicole were ready, we'd be allowed to jump down. Well, Maxi, being little, usually got lifted down. After that, we had to sit again and wait for our humans to close the car. This was hard for me. I was surrounded by new sights, sounds and smells, all of which I wanted to explore right there and then. Plus, I was always a little excited. No surprises there; I'm an excitable dog.

Sometimes I wondered if the humans made me wait till I had calmed down a bit. I'm not sure, but sometimes we'd all just hang around at the back of the car, the humans babbling away to each other. Whatever they were up to, my excitement had usually worn off a little before we set off.

We'd pass between some buildings and emerge into some sort of wide passage. There were people everywhere, though they tended to be either side of slightly raised footpaths of some sort. In the middle, cars were going both ways. It was pretty crowded. There were lots of smells here including those left by other dogs. These smells would grab my attention, and I would try to head off to explore them.

I never got far. I was always brought to heel. Next, we'd walk a bit, weaving our way through the crowd. Adrian seemed to be able to navigate through all these humans without bumping into them. I desperately wanted to get loose and meet and greet these people, explore all these smells, but I was kept under close control. The lead was loose, but Adrian was fast and any time I tried to move off, he would tighten the lead, bring me back and repeat the human bark, "Heel." In time, I just did as I was told; it was easier I suppose.

It was a mass of swirling movement and energies. Lots of the people seemed pretty stressed; I didn't like that. I was glad Adrian and Nicole always kept calm, as it made it easier to follow them. Sometimes I'd have to sit with Maxi and Adrian while Nicole disappeared into a building. Humans call these buildings "shops". It gave me a chance to take in some of the sights and smells. Ideally, I'd have liked to wander off and explore a bit, maybe see if any of the other dogs around wanted to play. But I was kept in a sitting position. If I tried to get up, I was always blocked straight away and made to sit.

Occasionally, we'd all go into a café where Adrian and Nicole would have something to eat and drink. Maxi and I would stretch out under the table. I'd position my head so I could watch the door. I liked watching the door; there was always something happening. If a dog came through, I might lift my head a little to get a better look. Most of the time, I just lay there happily drinking in the sights and smells.

Outside, in the street, the hardest part was walking past other dogs. It was different from the country walks. On those, the humans would usually stop and chat to each other. That would give me a chance to greet any dogs they might have. On these town walks, I had to walk straight past. I hardly had time to turn my head, let alone smell them and find out more about them. That said, I did enjoy these walks. While sitting outside shops, I often got attention from strange humans. Quite often, they'd babble away to me in their impenetrable language. I just smiled my best doggie smile and wagged my tail.

To be honest, I never felt the impulse to rush on these walks. There was so much going on that my head would be in a bit of a spin. It was easier just to follow Adrian.

Not all town walks were like that. Sometimes we'd walk through all the crowded areas and then turn into a passage that was quieter. Occasionally I'd hear little dogs yapping at windows. I ignored them. Some town walks turned into country walks. Adrian and Nicole seemed to like a walk that took us up a hill to see a building at the top of it. We used to pass sheep on that walk. I was always put on the lead. I wasn't sure why. I love sheep, and I could have gone and licked their bottoms clean (I really like doing that), but I never got the chance.

As we got closer to the top of this hill, it would get more crowded. At the top, there would be lots of humans of all sizes and usually a few dogs. Some of these dogs were running free. I was desperate to join them, but I was always kept on my lead. It was most frustrating. I'd try my usual tricks, including making lots of whiney noises to let Adrian and Nicole know that I wanted to play. That never worked. If I was sitting, I'd get up and look pointedly at where I wanted to go. That never worked. If I was walking alongside Adrian or Nicole, I'd pull in the direction I wanted to go. That never worked either.

Once, I couldn't take it any longer, and I lurched towards what looked like a really playful dog. This pulled Adrian over and he landed on a concrete step. Next second, I was flat on my back; Adrian's hand was on my chest and he was growling at me. It only lasted seconds. I understood; he was reminding me who was boss.

OK, I thought, and I gave in. While that made things a bit easier, I did find some parts of these walks hard. That said, over the years, I have learnt to follow Adrian's and Nicole's directions – most of the time. The fact is, every time we went to town, we went through the same routines and I got used to them. On walks, Adrian and Nicole were the leaders. Accepting this made things easier. Sometimes I'd even be let off the lead for spells, sometimes even with another dog.

Although these town walks were different from the walks near our house, I enjoyed them a lot.

Getting Attention

I've talked a lot about walks, as they are one of my favourite things. However, I also like attention. What dog doesn't? This attention can take many forms, including pats, back scratches, treats or even just an acknowledging look. Whatever it is, we dogs love it.

Dogs are brilliant at working out how to get attention from humans. We do this in a number of ways, but mainly by trying things out to see what works. We have lots of things we can try. A common one is jumping up. This is a puppy behaviour. As puppies, we get food from adult dogs by jumping up and licking their mouths. It works well with humans. Jump up, get in their faces and you can get anything from a pat through to a tasty morsel to eat.

Another is to wander over and stick our noses into whatever they are doing. That's a pretty good one, though it can be a bit risky. Variations of that include standing in front of the human and staring, pawing at them or even leaning on them. We can do cute things like rolling on our backs or rising up on our hind haunches like a squirrel. Other approaches such as barking or whining can have mixed results.

As a vocal dog, I am (or was) inclined to use the barking or whining approach a lot. I did, however, like jumping up or nudging humans (kind of leaning into them). I talk about jumping up elsewhere, but this is what happened when I used these strategies with Adrian and Nicole. To set the scene, you need to be aware that I have a jealous streak: I hate it when Adrian or Nicole give their attention elsewhere, especially to another dog.

Not long after I moved in with these humans, I was lying on the floor not far from Maxi. Nicole came over, sat down next to Maxi and started talking to her and giving her pats. I was instantly beside myself with jealousy. I went straight over, sat down next to Nicole and leant into her. Leaning in is a dog method of claiming something, and I was claiming Nicole. Being a big dog, my weight caused Nicole to move over a bit. She turned to look at me. I had got her attention away from Maxi. *Job done*, I thought. It's a good strategy with humans, the leaning in one. They often mistake it for affection. We dogs know it's dominance. But Nicole didn't realise that I was getting her attention by dominating her. I was getting her to do what I wanted. This was working fine until Adrian appeared. He said something to the female human and next thing, she had moved me away and went back to giving all her attention to Maxi.

With the lean-in strategy having worked once, I tried again. However, this time, she just stood up, grabbed my collar, led me away and went back to Maxi. I tried again – same result. I gave in and lay down, watching with my green eyes blazing. After a while, I dozed off. All of a sudden, I was getting pats. This was a bit of a puzzle. When I had leant in, I got sent away. When I did nothing, I got attention.

I had other tricks up my sleeve, and it wasn't long before I had another opportunity. Adrian and Nicole were sitting on their couch. I'd given up trying to sit on it now and had accepted that it was their couch, not mine. I felt like getting some attention, so I started whining. I have a pretty good whine, even if I say so myself. It's not high pitched and irritating – it's quite mellow and melodic. It floats up and down, and loudens and softens.

Adrian and Nicole didn't react at all. I kept going. Still nothing! This was strange – surely they could hear me. But no matter how hard I tried, they didn't even look at me, let alone come over and give me attention. I must have been at it for at least half an hour before I finally gave up. I dozed off and, sure enough, I got some attention soon after.

A few days later, I had another opportunity. I was outside in the garden. Adrian was busy laying flat stones. He was focused on his task and not paying me much attention. I wandered over hoping for a pat, but I got no reaction. I gave up and went to look for Nicole. Nicole was indoors and the door was shut. I thought I'd try and get some attention from her. I stood near the door and whined.

Nothing happened. I carried on whining. Still nothing.

I stopped whining and went round to look at Adrian. He didn't even acknowledge me. I went back to the door and whined for what seemed like ages, but nothing happened. Neither Adrian nor Nicole were deaf, so whining was not going to work. After a while, I stopped whining and found a comfortable spot to lie down. I never tried whining again; I had learnt that it was a waste of effort.

That said, what I have found that works is my greeting bark. It's not really a straight bark; for example, like a "woof". It's kind of a fusion of barky noises and whines, a sort of "wooh-wooh-wooh". I usually use this when I haven't seen a human that I know for a while. It works really well with the humans who live in houses nearby.

While there was fencing all around our last house and garden, here, in our current abode, it is much more open. There are no fences between the houses, so we can head right over to the next-door neighbours. Often, we dogs are allowed to wander around freely. If a neighbour human is out and about, I give my greeting bark, and that leads to them giving me lots of pats and attention. I have also found it very effective in getting visiting tradespeople to give me their lunch.

With Adrian and Nicole, I have found the best way to get attention is by lying down nearby. Sometimes rolling on my back does the trick. Truth be told, I don't really try and demand attention anymore, as it never works. I get enough attention just by be being me, so that's what I do.

The Picking Apples Game

We had a pretty big garden in our first abode – a wide area of grass with some trees, a pond and a couple of fields. When I was outside in this garden, I could pretty much do as I liked. Activities included lying down and watching the world go by, wandering around checking for new smells and watching the hens mooch about. Sometimes, I even rounded up the hens and took them back to their run.

Now and then I observed, through the fence, the yappy wee terriers that lived next door. I could have rushed them and told them off, but I kind of knew not to. It was better just to lie there and pretend they didn't exist. They usually gave up their yapping fairly quickly and wandered off into their own patch. In this garden, I came to invent a really good game: picking apples.

I found out about apples by accident. One day, I was out and about and found these round things lying on the ground. At first, I thought they were tennis balls and was about to ignore them but then I caught their smell. *Definitely not balls*, I thought. On closer inspection, they were sort of round but a bit lumpy. I popped one in my mouth. It wasn't meat, but it was kind of tasty. Humans call these things "apples". There were a few lying around, but some of them smelt mouldy or tangy, and I didn't fancy eating those.

The thing is, I noticed that there were more of these apples hanging from branches in the trees. With not a lot else to do, I wandered over, rocked back onto my haunches and stretched up. I found I could reach some of the apples that way. I took one in my mouth and pulled.

It pulled back.

I pulled harder and harder until it came away. *I won*, I thought to myself. It was a tug of war game – what fun! I

76

managed to pull a few more off the branches before something else grabbed my attention. I remembered this new game and how much fun it was.

A few days later, we were all out in the garden and I was bored. I decided to play the apple picking game. I wandered over to a tree and looked up. I selected my target apple and got ready to pick it. As I was reaching to grab the apple, I heard my name being called. I dropped down and looked around to find Adrian looking at me and saying, "No." I understood by now that "no" meant I was not to do what I was doing, so I did as I was told and wandered off.

What this experience taught me was that I should only play the apple picking game when Adrian and Nicole could not see me. This worked and I managed to play it a few times. I would walk down to an apple tree and find a target apple. Then I'd look around to see if any humans were watching me. If they were, I'd wander off and lie down. If not, I'd have a second look. I was very deliberate about this; I did not want to get caught. Once I was sure no human could see me, I'd reach up and pull an apple from the tree. I got a real buzz from doing this.

One day, we were all in the garden. Adrian and Nicole were busy and not paying much attention to me. In fact, Nicole had gone back inside and Adrian was in one of the outbuildings. I looked around for another check. The coast was clear. I wandered over to a tree and selected my target apple. It hung invitingly on a branch not far above my head. Standing there, I looked around to my right. All clear. I looked around to my left. All clear. Just to be sure, I did this again. All clear.

I rocked back on my haunches and started to rise up to the apple. Just as I started to rise, I heard a loud noise that made me jump out of my skin. Back on four feet again, I looked around. There was nobody there. It had sounded suspiciously like a human clapping, but there was no human in sight. I looked around to my right. All clear. I looked around to my left. All clear. Just to be sure, I did this again. All clear. I tried again, rocking back onto my haunches and starting to reach up. *CLAP!* I jumped out of my skin again. I looked around, but there were no humans in sight. In an instant, the apple picking game had gone from being fun to being frightening, so I decided to stop playing it. I went and lay down.

What I didn't know was that, while having excellent eyesight, we dogs don't take in stationary objects very well. We are designed to detect movement – it's a hunting skill. What I also didn't know was that Adrian knew this. He had spotted me heading towards the apple tree. All he had done was stand next to a large tree about 30 metres away. He was hiding in plain sight. When I looked around, he had stood motionless, and I just didn't see him.

I never played the apple picking game again.

Chasing Cyclists

By now, you might be getting an impression of what kind of a dog I am. I like to think I am pretty good natured. I mean, I have never bitten any human or any other dog. I like people and I like dogs. I am also pretty playful and have lots of energy. I am independent, and that means I sometimes don't listen to Adrian and Nicole when they tell me to do things, particularly when they call me back at times when I am enjoying myself.

Throughout my time with Nicole and Adrian, I have mostly done what I was told. That said, I have always been more inclined to follow Adrian's instructions. As well as being more assertive, he had more "dog" about him. By that, I mean he could use looks and body language that persuaded me to obey him, even if I didn't want to. He could also be quite adept at distracting me during key moments in a way that caused me to forget what I was doing, and I'd automatically do what he wanted instead.

On the other hand, Nicole used to be a lot easier to handle. I had worked out that if I arranged my mouth in a kind of human smile shape and gazed at her, she would go all soft and gooey and give me lots of attention. During the early years, I paid less attention to her commands and only really executed them if I felt like it. That said, she could be pretty strict on a heel walk.

All in all, when Adrian wasn't around, I used to assume leadership of the pack, but this all changed one day.

We (Nicole, Maxi and I) had just got back from a walk. It wasn't a play session with Bear and Luna, it was a country walk, and I still had some energy to burn. Maxi and I were sitting waiting for Nicole to open the gate. She needed both hands for this, so Maxi and I were sitting there off lead. Out of nowhere, a group of humans shot past on bicycles.

In a flash, I was off after them. It was brilliant. I had to run pretty fast to catch up, and then I dropped into a good lope to keep up with them. The cyclists didn't seem that bothered and kept going. I could hear Nicole calling my name, but I just ignored her. I was having too much fun.

Off we went down the road, around the double bend and up the hill. Eventually, we got far enough away that I started to feel a bit uncomfortable. I was also a bit puffed out now; it had been a long, full-on run. I am built for short bursts of speed, not long runs. I slowed down, turned and trotted back feeling very happy with myself. Nicole was waiting for me at the gate. She didn't seem very happy. I wondered what had happened to upset her. I felt like I could do with a pat, so I put on my dog smile. For the first time, it didn't work. I was puzzled. I wasn't doing anything wrong, was I? I thought she liked my dog smile. We walked back to the house. I was a little nervous; something in Nicole's demeanour felt threatening. When we got to the house, I made straight for my bed and lay down.

It was after that that things changed. Nicole became

more like Adrian. By that, I mean she became both more assertive and more like a dog, more like a pack leader. I found that I was no longer able to take control when Adrian was away. I was fine with that; most dogs would be really. If we have a good pack leader, we are happy to follow. The upshot of it all was that my feelings didn't change; I still loved her unreservedly. But I found a new level of respect for her.

Another strange thing was that Adrian seemed to relax a bit more. It was as if he was happier now that Nicole was also a pack leader. It was around then that I came to accept them as the alpha male and female.

I was fine with that. Up to a point.

Barking at Everything

Author's note: Controlling barking is something that is all too easy for humans to be inconsistent at. We can train dogs to be quiet on command, but we are generally poor at enforcing this in a consistent manner – sometimes we can let them bark for a while before asking them to be quiet. Other times we can say "quiet" straight away, possibly in irritation when they've given us a fright. A lot of the time we, as humans, completely misinterpret why they are barking in the first place.

Our goal with George was to allow him to bark as a guard dog, but to stop him barking when we asked. We never achieved this. The traditional training methods and dog psychology approaches may work with some breeds, but they didn't with George.

What we learnt is that barking is core to George's breed. It's deeply rooted in Anatolian shepherds to bark at everything, either as an alert, a warning or as a greeting. At first, we tended just to hear barking, but over time we have come to realise that George has a vast range of barks. For example, every delivery van gets a different bark.

This is not a breed you want to have in a highly populated area.

My breed, the Anatolian shepherd, originates from Turkey and Greece, and is that of a livestock guard dog. My role is to live with my livestock and to keep them safe from predators such as wolves and bears. I do this in a number of ways, but my primary approach is by barking. I have a range of barks that mean different things. My sheep seem to understand my barks perfectly. Adrian and Nicole do not. I shall do my best to try and explain, but you must remember that dog logic and human logic are quite different.

I have a wide and complex range of barks. At the risk of simplifying things, these fall loosely into three categories: "alert", "warning" and "greeting". I use alert barks when I detect a problem somewhere, perhaps a sheep is in trouble or something is happening towards the edge of my territory. The latter could be a neighbour walking their dog, for example. Warning barks are a higher level. I use these when I detect a threat, usually close by. The main purpose of these barks is to scare the threat away, thus avoiding a fight, but I will charge while barking if the threat gets too close. Greeting barks are for when I meet someone I know.

In each of these categories there can be quite a few variations, with each bark having subtle differences and nuances depending on, for example, the time of day, what I've detected, whether I've detected it before, and so on. Sometimes I think the humans can't tell the difference.

In this life, I am not a livestock guardian dog. I live with humans in a house along with other dogs. Yes, I have sheep and hens here, but while I love being with them and sometimes helping when the sheep are moved from one area to another, I am only occasionally left with them for guarding duties. I do not live out with them in the fields. Also, as I've not had a dog or human train me on how to guard livestock, I'm not sure how I would cope if I found myself living out in the fields with the sheep. In effect, I am between two worlds: that of the humans and that of guardian of the sheep.

Don't get me wrong, I am perfectly happy with this arrangement. However, this situation is fertile ground for misunderstandings between Adrian, Nicole and myself. First off, living with humans as I do, my instincts translate into guarding our patch, our territory. It is important to understand that what I perceive as our territory does not necessarily coincide with human boundaries, such as walls and fences. It is an area that I feel I need to protect. For example, here in our Scottish residence, my area of interest stretches well into neighbouring farms and land.

In my original role as an Anatolian shepherd, I would be living outside. I would assess potential threats in an instinctual way – the sorts of sights and sounds that might trigger fight or flight responses. These would be noises made by bears, wolves, other dogs and humans, for example, approaching through woodland or grasslands. Being in a human world, there is a much wider range of things going on. It is my role to bark at anything and everything that I feel could be a threat to our territory.

Such situations include things like a person going past the gate, a cyclist on the road nearby, a horse and rider passing by, a dog barking somewhere, a dog in a nearby garden, a cat anywhere nearby, people coming up the drive, people knocking on the door, children playing nearby, a neighbouring farmer at work, a neighbour's car engine, a delivery van approaching, a deer passing by in the early hours, a fox passing by at night, and so on. On top of that, when I'm out in the fields while Adrian and Nicole are checking on the sheep, I naturally drop into guard mode. Anything happening within range needs to be barked at – from a crow alighting too close, to a quad bike on the other side of the valley.

Over time, as I learn what is a threat and what is not, my barks evolve to match the situation. Sometimes I will be alerting Adrian and Nicole, sometimes I will be warning the threat to back off, sometimes I will be greeting the intruder.

The time of day also makes a difference insofar as intrusions in the night are perceived as more threatening. Also, with Adrian and Nicole asleep, it is up to me to deal with the threat until they get up and take over. Night-time barks are usually louder and more prolonged.

For example, the postie gets an alert bark if I'm indoors, but a welcome bark if I'm outside. Some delivery vans get a full-on bark, some get a mild warning bark and others I just ignore as I recognise them. Nicole returning in her car may get a welcome bark, but maybe not. A neighbour's car door gets an alert bark during the day, but a warning bark during the night. The level of bark depends on whether I recognise the sound made by the car's engine or door opening/closing. However you look at it, it's a lot of barking. The thing is, my barking doesn't always seem to go down well with Adrian and Nicole.

As I have said, Adrian and Nicole are pretty good at being dogs. But they're not perfect. While they have some understanding of us dogs and our psychology, they sometimes get their communications with us dogs wrong. One such area is barking. Adrian and Nicole have taught me a command: "quiet". I understand what "quiet" means. It means "stop barking". As with all dogs, I live entirely in the moment. Any command or stimulus I detect applies to what I am doing right there and then.

Take the situation where I've heard someone at the door, so I've started to bark. I then hear Adrian or Nicole say, "Quiet." In that moment, mid-barking, my dog logic interprets the command of "quiet" to mean that barking is not allowed. To me, it is simple: all barking is not allowed. However, simple as it may sound, this sets up a conflict with all my instincts.

Another situation might be when I detect something approaching from a distance, so I bark an alert bark. Adrian or Nicole would then tell me to be quiet. I stop barking; I have obeyed the quiet command. But then the intruder carries on approaching. The situation has now changed, so I have an overpowering urge to bark again, slightly louder. To be clear, this is not a continuation of my last bark; it is a new bark. This new bark doesn't seem to go down well.

Sometimes I bark if there is something just outside the house. I am told to be quiet. I obey the command and stop barking, but the intruder is still there, outside the house. The threat is still present. I can't help but bark again. For me, it is simple. If I detect an intruder, I bark until the intruder is dealt with or leaves. So strong is my guard instinct that I have to continue barking even though I know Adrian and Nicole have told me not to. This causes a conflict in me, leading to me feeling anxious.

On top of that, barking is core to my nature. Taking that away can lead to deeper anxiety and even nervous behaviour – for example, licking my paw.

These days, I am rarely asked to be quiet if I detect something. I bark, and Adrian or Nicole head off to investigate. I may bark a while longer, or I may feel I have barked enough. It's my call. I do watch Nicole and Adrian very carefully to see how they react, but lately they seem perfectly happy while I'm barking.

Perhaps Adrian and Nicole are beginning to understand. What's interesting is that I don't bark for very long now.

The key point is, even with dog-knowledgeable humans, miscommunication can still happen. And it's up to the humans to sort it.

Jumping Up

Why do we dogs jump up? Simple, we are seeking food. In the wild, the adult dogs will head off to hunt for food. Once they have killed something, the dogs are allowed to approach the kill in order of status. Basically, the alpha dogs feed first, then the next highest, and so on. If food is scarce, it can be difficult for lower-status dogs to get anything to eat. We dogs can get pretty aggressive defending our food and our position in the food chain. There can be occasional fights as hungry dogs try to sneak in for a bite out of turn.

Puppies, should they approach the kill, are tolerated by the adult dogs. They can sneak in and take tasty morsels no matter which adult dogs are feeding. But it can be a bit tricky pushing your way in when you are only a puppy. A better strategy is to get food directly from an adult. What tends to happen is that the adults will get in, tear themselves a piece of meat and head off to eat it in peace. What puppies then do is rush over to them and jump up and lick their mouths. Eventually, if they're persistent enough (and they usually are), the adult dog will give the jumping puppy some or all of its meat.

In the human world, we dogs need our humans to be dogs. We cannot be humans. We perceive the actions of humans as though they are two-legged dogs. When humans return from being away, our instinct is to get food from them. This is especially true when we are puppies because we are growing and need lots to eat. So, when our humans return, we jump up to get food. We are jumping up trying to get to their mouths. While I am pretty big and can reach a human mouth quite easily, some of the smaller dogs have to work really hard and jump really high.

You might ask if this is the case, why do adult dogs jump? There are two reasons: breeding and attention.

Over the years, humans have bred us selectively for all sorts of reasons. At first, it was to make better working dogs. Humans wanted dogs to guard them, fetch things for them, deal with their rodent problems, find things, drag their stuff around for them, even drag the humans around, keep their feet warm and catch dinner for them.

In our original wolf build, we were multiskilled. By that, I mean we were good all-rounders in terms of sight, hearing, smell, speed, guard instincts, and so on. Humans have created dogs of all different sizes and shapes to better carry out specific tasks for humans. Lately, the breeding has been more about what we look like. I don't get that. We dogs don't care what we look like. We never have – I mean, what's the point? Good looks don't get you dinner. Good looks don't get you status. Looks are irrelevant to us. So, what are the humans up to?

I digress.

The point I am trying to make is, amongst all this breeding, humans have also bred us, by accident or by design, to keep our puppy behaviours for longer. That's why adult dogs jump up, too; they are still puppies at heart.

Now, what I have noticed is that humans can misinterpret this jumping up as affection. They interpret the jumping as a dog's way of saying "I missed you" or something similar. This anthropomorphism (my humans use big words too) is not only wrong, it's not actually very good for the dog's mental health. Humans often reward the jumping dog with attention or food treats. In effect, the human has just trained us to jump up on any approaching human, as we now know that we can get rewarded with attention and food.

I was no different from most dogs. When I was adopted by Adrian and Nicole, I jumped up at them. It achieved nothing. What happened was that when I jumped up, Adrian and Nicole just turned their backs on me. In fact, they behaved as though I didn't exist. I've heard that ignoring someone is considered bad in the human world. Very rude, in fact. In the dog world, ignoring another dog is completely normal. It avoids unnecessary conflict. For example, if I ignore another dog, I am not perceived as a threat. In this moment, Adrian and Nicole were not behaving like humans; they were behaving like dogs. So, if you or another dog do something that irritates me, I will ignore you. It's the best way to get you to stop without things escalating.

Given this jumping up instinct is a food gatherī. exercise, it's a pretty strong instinct. It wasn't as if I jumped up once, got ignored and never did it again. I jumped up on humans many times over many months. Most of the time, this was on humans who came to visit us. They'd come in through the gate and head up the track towards our house. I'd rush over to them and plant my front paws on their shoulders. That way, I could get really close to their mouths to see if there was anything in there. Old or young, little or big, it made no difference. Come up my drive, my paws would end up on your shoulders.

Of course, Adrian or Nicole would usually be calling me but, to be honest, an approaching human is always going to be more interesting than a pat on the head. And it was early days – recall was not yet an automatic response. Not that it ever was, or is.

Once, an elderly lady was walking up the drive and I nearly knocked her over. Another time, our next-door neighbour (the one with all the Labradors) dropped by. I charged over, slightly misjudged my jump and careered into his leg, nearly breaking it. Adrian and Nicole started to intervene more decisively. I subsequently found that when I jumped up, not only would I be ignored, I would be led away by Adrian or Nicole (whoever was closest). If indoors, I'd be put in my bed. If outdoors, I'd be locked in the house for a few minutes.

Over time, Adrian and Nicole began to intercept or distract me before I got to the visiting human. They would make me sit and wait. If I did so, I'd get lots of attention. It took a while but, over time, I jumped up less and less. These days I don't jump up at all. I just do my welcome bark, which seems to work pretty well at getting me attention.

All in all, I think Adrian, Nicole and I have worked out a good compromise here.

tioned, we dogs live in the moment. What's
ie past. What has not yet happened is not
about. There is only now. Like all creatures,
there are occasionally seismic events that make a massive
difference to our lives. If I were able to look back, I suspect
being found in that cardboard box was one of them. Being
adopted by Nicole and Adrian might be another. But, by far
the biggest, I think, was when I was accepted by
DogiPlayce.

So, I hear you ask, what is DogiPlayce? DogiPlayce is a
place where humans can leave their dog for a period. You
can leave your dog for the day, or even days or weeks. It is a
well-run place staffed by humans who are pretty good at
being dogs. At DogiPlayce, all the dogs are allowed to run
together in a big field under the supervision of a human.
Dogs have to be assessed for their suitability before they're
accepted. Places are at a premium. Prior to my first visit, I
knew none of this.

One day, myself and Maxi were bundled into the car.
Great, I thought, *adventure awaits*. I sat there with my dog grin
splashed all over my face. Maxi had her usual car scowl, but
I was too busy looking out of the window to pay much
attention to that. We arrived at a new place, somewhere I
had not been before. We went through the usual
disembarkation procedures and I was put on a lead. My
goodness, the smells that hit me were amazing. I could
smell so many dogs. I could hear dogs, and it sounded like a
lot of them were playing. I couldn't help a whimper of
excitement escaping from my mouth.

Unbeknown to me, we had arrived at DogiPlayce.

I was torn between doing what I was told and rushing
towards the dogs. I couldn't see them as they were the
other side of a high fence, but I could hear and smell them,
so I knew exactly where they were. As Adrian had me on a

short lead, I had no choice but to walk to heel. I could sense that he meant business so, hard as it was, I did what I was told. Maxi was with Nicole.

We passed through some gates. We were getting closer to the dogs. I was almost wetting myself with excitement. We stopped on this big concrete area surrounded by an iron fence. On the other side, there was a grassy field full of dogs running around. Adrian made me sit. I can't even begin to explain how hard that was. Just metres from me, a large pack of dogs were playing. It evoked memories of the rescue centre. I was desperate to join them, but I had to sit.

Adrian and Nicole were chatting to the DogiPlayce staff. All the time I had to sit. All I wanted to do was go and meet these dogs. I sat there for what seemed like an eternity, small whimpers of frustration escaping from my lips. Finally, after what seemed like an eternity of sitting, Adrian started leading me towards the gate into the field full of dogs. I was still on a heel, I think. I was caught between wanting to please Adrian and my desire to charge into the melee.

At the gate, he passed my lead to one of the DogiPlayce staff humans. I didn't really notice to tell you the truth; my attention was on all the dogs. I was led into the field by this new human. He, too, kept me on a short lead. Dogs started coming over to smell me and check me out. Loving other dogs, as I do, I was as friendly as I could be. I waved my head around and tried to lick their faces while all the time wagging my tail for all it was worth. I couldn't do a full dog greeting because I was still on the lead.

Then, all of a sudden, the DogiPlayce staff human leant down and released me. I needed no second invitation. I was off like a shot, flat out in a run. In an instant, other dogs were running with me. I changed direction, and they followed me. We were all playing flat out. It was brilliant. I didn't even notice the DogiPlayce staff human wander off back to join the other humans. I just ran and ran and ran. I did swerves, body checks, play bows – the lot. We were all pretty big dogs. Some didn't join in. Some played for a bit. I didn't stop – it was play, play and more play.

It was the start of something big. I didn't know it, but DogiPlayce had been assessing me. Being a big dog and an unusual breed, they needed to see how I would interact with the other dogs there. Unknown to me, I had passed with flying colours. Anyway, I was allowed to play for quite a long time before I was taken home. I was a happy dog. I was also pretty tired, so I had a good sleep. In the coming months, I had the occasional day at DogiPlayce. It was always brilliant.

One day, Adrian took Maxi and I to DogiPlayce. This day, he joined us in the field. I was off playing straight away. I had my favourites, and we would run and run and play and play. Adrian would walk around the field watching all the dogs. Truth be told, there were a few unbalanced dogs in there – some you could write a book about. I wondered why they were like that. Maybe their humans were not very good dogs. Who knows? The worst were a couple of Labradors. I gave them a wide berth.

We started to go there every second day or so. It was just brilliant. We'd be there straight after breakfast, play for hours, then we'd be taken home and I'd sleep for a couple of days until it was DogiPlayce time again. This was while I was still less than three years old. I was still a puppy really. A big puppy, but basically a big play dog. During that time, I had everything I needed: plenty of exercise, lots of time with other dogs, discipline and heaps of affection. It was just perfect.

There were a lot of dogs in that play field and they came in all shapes and sizes. There was everything from small terriers to Rhodesian ridgebacks (about the same size as me). Yet, even with all those dogs, it was amazingly calm. What I mean is that there were many random dogs thrown together into what was not an established pack. The potential for disagreement was high. Adrian seemed to have an instinct for where trouble was breaking out. He would spot something in a dog's body language and just move in to separate and distract them. He kept the energy amongst the dogs pretty calm. I mean, there was a lot of play energy, but that was fun energy.

I still got to play with Bear and Luna some days too. I have to admit that if I bumped into Bear and Luna just after getting back from DogiPlayce, I might not have been quite as playful. I was worn out. But when we met on other days, we still had a good run around.

DogiPlayce went on for a long time. One day, though, we moved to a new place far away called Scotland, so we stopped going to DogiPlayce.

Counter Surfing

It was the middle of winter and it was cold and wet outside. Indoors, it was nice and warm and I was lying in my bed. We had strangers staying in the house with us, and I was getting lots of attention and enjoying every minute. Adrian and Nicole had planted a tree in the corner of the room and covered it in brightly coloured baubles and lights. I had given it a quick check, but it was of little interest to me. In this particular moment, all the humans were sitting in their chairs babbling away in human. I lay in my bed and studied them.

I was distracted by an amazing smell that wafted over. I can't describe it – all I can say is that it smelt of food. Not just food, though. It was the most amazing food I have ever smelt. I was torn. Do I stay in bed or do I investigate? I knew human food was out of bounds, but the smell was just too enticing. The smell was coming from the kitchen. Above the kitchen cupboards there was a wooden platform they called a counter. It was just about level with my head. I knew I wasn't allowed to investigate these counters. I had learnt that investigating these counters was risky.

Once, in my younger years, not long after I'd moved here, Adrian and Nicole had gone outside. I went to investigate the smells on these counters. I didn't find any food, but I did find a small dish with something unusual in it. They were little red pod-like things. Having found nothing else to eat, I tried some of these. I don't know what they were, but my mouth was on fire for hours afterwards. It put me off surfing those counters, I can tell you.

That evening, the smell was overpowering and I lay there just drinking it in. I studied the humans and saw that they were all busy with one another. I made my decision. Stealthily, I got up and padded across the floor. I noticed Adrian watching me, but he made no move. Maybe he thought I was heading to my water bowl. I slunk out of his view into the kitchen. In front of me, just above my head, was a big, brown, tasty-looking morsel. It looked like a big bird with no feathers. The smell was overpowering. I moved closer, approaching it slowly and stealthily. I got ready to rise up and grab it with my mouth. Just as my jaws were about to close on it, just as I was about to sink my teeth into this amazing morsel, I heard my name barked out from behind me. I turned and saw Adrian standing there looking at me. He pointed at me and then swung his hand to point at my bed. I got the message and went scurrying back to my bed.

It's hard being a dog sometimes. There are all these smells that I want to investigate. Instinctively, I know that Adrian's and Nicole's food is out of bounds, mainly because they are the alpha dogs in our pack. To me, rules are more like guidelines. As far as I was concerned, it was perfectly fine for me to try and steal some of their food if I thought I could get away with it.

The humans always ate their meals at another raised platform: a table. From day one, the humans had made it clear that I could not approach this table. That was fine; they were the alpha dogs. As I said, it is in our nature as dogs not to interrupt the alpha dogs when they are eating. To be honest, it made life much easier for me. I never had the constant anxiety of wondering if I'd get any of my humans' food. Sometimes I did, in my normal meals. Overall, this arrangement worked for me.

That said, the independent streak in me sometimes emerged. One day there were strangers visiting. Adrian and Nicole had put a lot of food out. Some on the table and some on the kitchen counters. Odours of ham wafted across my nose. I lay in bed, as usual, and watched. Suddenly, all the humans went out into the garden. I lay in my bed and observed. I waited a while, but the humans didn't reappear, so I decided to investigate. I found the cold meat on a plate on the table and I ate it. It was lovely. I went back to my bed and lay down.

Eventually, the humans came back. They looked a bit puzzled, and I sensed from their body language that they were a bit unhappy about something. At first, they could not work out where the meat had gone. Then, as one, they turned and looked at me. I looked right back. I was in my bed and in that moment, I was behaving perfectly. The humans sat down and ate. I lay there contentedly.

Another time, I found a spicy sausage on the table. I carefully picked it up and took it back to my bed. I got it between my paws and was about to bite into it when Nicole appeared. She came straight over and took it off me. Oh well, that was her right as alpha female. Pity – it had smelt rather delicious.

Generally, when other humans are in the house and there is food laid out, we dogs just lie in our beds and watch. We are quite content because, in the world of dogs, we understand the concept of unavailable food. All food belongs to the alpha dogs, and they share it with us as per the hierarchy. What we have learnt is that when the house is full of humans and we stay in our beds, we get lots of attention. That makes it tempting to stay in our beds because we love attention.

However, in the world of dogs, when any dog leaves its food, even for an instant, that food is fair game. If we can, we will snatch the food even if it "belongs" to the alpha dog. So if, for example, the humans put food out and leave the room, I may try to take the food. The humans may be alpha dogs, but we dogs will take our chances; and if there's a chance to scavenge some food, then scavenge we will. It's what we do.

Beds and Humans

Adrian and Nicole have provided us dogs with our own beds. They are kind of fluffy, full of soft padding and pretty comfortable. I like my bed. I also like sleeping on the floor, especially if I'm feeling a bit hot. The floor is always nice and cool. I also like stretching out in front of the fire when it has been lit. So, you might be wondering why I mention beds at all. Well, there are a couple of things.

If I stretch right out, I am much bigger than my bed. In fact, my bed is not much bigger than my torso. So, if I stretch out, my legs, head and tail are all on the floor. That doesn't really bother me; I am still pretty comfortable. The other problem is the other dogs. Maxi was already living here when I arrived. Haribo joined us later. What often happens is that I head over to my bed only to find Maxi or Haribo already in it. Now, I know I'm supposed to be top dog and I know that Maxi and Haribo should give way to me, but they don't. To be honest, I am not sure what to do.

Sometimes I look around, and Adrian or Nicole spot the problem and move the offending dog back into their own bed. I am always pretty thankful for that. That said, I have tried Maxi's tiny bed out for size once or twice. I find that if

I curl up really tight and tuck my legs in, I can just about fit. It makes my humans laugh.

Adrian and Nicole have a big bed, big enough even for me, but I am not allowed on that. None of us dogs are – it's a humans-only bed.

One day a visitor (Nicole's brother Matt) came to stay. We liked him; he gave us lots of pats. Maxi would follow him everywhere with an adoring look on her face, but that's another story. At that time, in our house, Adrian and Nicole's bed was in an upstairs room. We used to sleep next to the bed, but one day we were moved out to the passage next to their room. That was fine with me; I was happy to sleep anywhere so long as it was not too far from my humans. Our beds were downstairs, but Nicole had thoughtfully put beds upstairs too. We could sleep upstairs or downstairs as we felt.

Matt was given a bed downstairs. In fact, the sofa had somehow been changed into a bed. Now, that was interesting. We dogs were not allowed on the sofa. I had tried to circumvent this rule a few times with no luck. But now, the sofa was no longer a sofa. It was a big, flat, soft area that looked like a bed. I wondered if I'd be allowed on it. This situation also presented me with a conundrum. Do I sleep upstairs like I usually do, or do I sleep downstairs near Matt?

When the humans went to bed, I lay on the floor downstairs and waited. Once it was dark, I got up and walked over to this new bed. It looked perfect. I jumped up on it and lay down. It was bliss. As well as being a big soft area, there was some sort of fluffy blanket. I stretched right out, taking up most of the available space. I could feel Matt lying there too. That was fine; we could share. I had a blissful night's sleep. Next day, Matt seemed a bit out of sorts.

The next evening, things changed a bit. At human bedtime, Matt sat on the edge of the sofa bed. His body language was very different. Last night he had been all cuddly and gooey with me at bedtime. Tonight, he sat on that bed as though he owned it. I wasn't quite sure what to make of this, so I lay down on the floor for a while. When it had been dark for a while, I got up and jumped up onto the bed. This time, Matt got up and dragged me off by my collar. I hadn't been expecting that. I waited for Matt to fall asleep and tried again. Once again, I was removed from the bed.

So, it was Matt's bed now. OK, I got the message and lay down on the floor and went to sleep.

Sheep

When I was first adopted by Nicole and Adrian, the only animals they had were the hens. A few months later, three sheep arrived. The sheep and I had a formal introduction supervised by Adrian. I believe Adrian's intention was to ensure that I knew my place in the scheme of things insofar as the sheep were higher status and were therefore to be treated with respect. Adrian and Nicole needn't have worried; my instinct told me that these were the very creatures I had been bred to protect.

Of course, the sheep did not know this. To them, I was a wolf and they were very wary of me. That was fine. I instinctively knew how to handle them, and I let them get used to me. In due course, more sheep arrived; I had to let them get to know me too. Adrian and Nicole helped by taking me with them to the flock on their routine checks. Over time, the sheep came to accept me and even let me groom them.

In the following spring, Adrian and Nicole were very busy with the sheep. Over a few weeks, lambs started appearing. I loved those lambs straight away. Two came to live with us in the house. They were orphan lambs. They had their own enclosure but were allowed to wander freely when Adrian and Nicole were around. I watched out for them.

Some of the lambs had problems with their poos. Adrian and Nicole showed me the problem, and I licked the lambs' bottoms clean. I did a far better job than the humans could have done. I loved helping like that. Later, when the lambs were taken out of the shed and into the field, I found myself being left in the field with them. I was torn between my guard instinct and the fact that I was a pet, but my instinct won and I watched over the lambs and their mothers. No fox was getting near my flock.

When we moved to Scotland, three new sheep appeared. They were not happy to see me, let me tell you, and they tried to biff me whenever I went near. It took a while, but slowly they came to accept me, too. In fact, one of them, Ursi, and I have become good friends. She often seeks me out so that I can groom her.

Here in Scotland we have much more space. The sheep wander freely over a large area. I get to see them at least three times a day. Sometimes I help out a bit. Adrian and Nicole occasionally move the sheep from one area to another. They lead the sheep rather than rounding them up. The sheep are quite happy to follow, but often there are one or two stragglers. I take up position at the rear to make sure they are OK. I like doing that.

I have noticed that it's only our flock of sheep that I am allowed to be near. Where we live, there are other sheep nearby. Sometimes they are in the fields right next to my patch. I am not allowed to visit them. Sometimes, I really want to go and lick their faces, but it never happens. Occasionally we go on trips away from here, and one of those trips takes us to some hills. There are sheep everywhere there. Us dogs are always put on leads around these other sheep. Now, you might think that I would never chase them or that I hate being on the lead.

You'd be wrong on both counts.

I love our sheep. I would never hurt them. But I am a dog, descended from wolves. Like all dogs, I have the instinct to hunt. Where I live, there are all sorts of furry creatures. We see rabbits, hares, pheasants, ducks and sometimes even deer. I can smell rats, mice, moles and voles everywhere. If I detect a hare or a deer, my natural instinct is to run after it. In fact, if I see any animal running away, I feel compelled to chase it – I can't help it. One look from Adrian can stop me in my tracks, but I am not always looking at my humans. If I don't see them warning me not to and a hare or deer runs past, I will be off after it. This extends to all furry creatures. Adrian and Nicole know that even though I love sheep, if I see one running away, my hunting instinct might kick in. So, as a dog, there is always a risk I will run after something, even humans (especially on bicycles).

I am happy to be on the lead. Yes, it might be a new and exciting place and there might be lots of exciting smells, but, if my human wants me on a lead, I am happy to follow. I know my place, and I respect Adrian and Nicole.

As I may have mentioned, my key needs as a dog (exercise, discipline and affection) are being fulfilled. The sheep add that bit extra as they enable me to be my breed, for want of a better expression. I love my time with the sheep, watching out for them and grooming them. It's the icing on my life's cake.

On Reflection

I have a great life. I live with Adrian and Nicole, another dog (Haribo) on a small farm with sheep and chickens. I have grown to understand my humans and, better still, they have grown to understand me. It took a while. Many of the experiences I have written about took place in my first two or three years of living with Adrian and Nicole. After that, I think I got the hang of the rules, and also Adrian and Nicole got the hang of me. It wasn't always easy; I was big, excitable, full of energy and not inclined to do what I was told.

I get plenty of exercise through walks and play. We have a collie that lives nearby and sometimes I play with her. We love charging through the trees. Haribo joins in occasionally if he's in the mood. The two collies prefer to play ball, though. Fetching a ball is not my cup of tea. That said, when I am in the mood, I muscle in on the ball game and snatch it away from the collies. I stand there mouthing it, which drives them nuts. They just want to play "fetch", but I have their ball. They have to chase me to try and get it back, which involves lots of running around.

I have discipline, though I have to admit that I can find this hard at times. As an independent breed, my instinct is to make decisions on my own. Sometimes I make those decisions when I think danger threatens my patch, usually an intruder approaching the front door. But I also feel I have to alert Adrian and Nicole when there are things around, such as a cat outside, a deer passing in the small hours, our neighbouring humans getting back late, that sort of thing.

I also have a natural tendency to lead. I must be a natural because I find many dogs want to follow me. Sometimes I just click into being pack leader, which means I start doing my own thing more and listening to Adrian and Nicole less. For example, on the walk I'll wander off and start looking for moles or something like that. In that moment, I'll ignore any recall commands I hear. If my humans sense I am taking over, they will become more assertive and take back control. They make pretty good dogs, so I am usually happy to comply. They understand that what makes a human leader is entirely different from what makes a good dog pack leader.

It's a delicate balance, but I think we have got it about right.

This leadership issue demonstrates that the relationship between human and dog is always changing, always adjusting. Adrian and Nicole understand that looking after a dog involves far more than a few trips to puppy school and the odd bit of training. They have to behave like dogs every minute of every day. They have to maintain control at all times. They have to be aware that we dogs are independent, sentient creatures who can think for ourselves and that our logic is completely different. They also have to be aware that however clever they might think they are, we dogs are likely to take advantage as and when we can.

This last point is important. You might not like to hear it, but I like to hunt. Our fields are awash with furry creatures of all sorts: mice, voles, moles and even hares. If I get the chance, I will hunt, kill and eat them. I know my humans don't want me to do this. However, if they are not looking, for example, busy with the sheep, I will take my chances. Adrian and Nicole are wise to this, and they watch me like a hawk. But, sometimes, they get distracted.

I get affection, and this comes in many forms. Of course, there are the pats and strokes, and I like those a lot. The humans talk to us and although we never know what they're saying, the music of the words is pleasant. We can feel that they are happy with us, and that makes us happy. We are well looked after.

Further afield, I have great human neighbours. They always seem pleased to see me and they always give me pats. We have three houses nearby, and I get on with all the humans. Sometimes these humans have visitors and I get pats from them too.

So, summarising, I am lucky to have humans that treat me and respect me as a dog. That's really important. We dogs are ill-suited to being treated like baby humans, princesses or teddy bears. Such treatment makes us anxious, and there's a fine line between anxiety and aggression. It's all too easy for us dogs to become unbalanced when we are not respected as dogs. That's when the problems can start. We dogs need our humans to be dogs. We need them to be in control. We need them to be good pack leaders. If they are not, we have to take over, and that doesn't always turn out too well.

Kika

Author's note: Kika's owner (Nicole's mother) had to go into hospital for an operation, and she had been advised to allow at least seven weeks for recovery. During that period, walking Kika would have been impossible. We offered to look after Kika until she was ready, and our offer was gratefully accepted.

Hi, I'm Kika and I'm a Spanish mongrel (from Cadiz) with a bit of terrier, water dog and sighthound all mixed together. I'm brown all over, a kind of rich chocolate brown, and about the size of a collie. I have bright, bushy eyebrows that make me look quite fierce, but I'm actually quite gentle really. I can't remember much about my time in Spain; it seems like a lifetime ago. All I remember is that one day I was bundled into a crate and left there for what seemed like days. Yes, I was moving. Well, I wasn't moving (being in the crate), the contraption I was in was moving.

Finally, I got somewhere and was let out. I was greeted by a female human I had never seen before, but she acted as if I was her long-lost best friend. I was slightly disconcerted by this stranger but, at the same time, I loved the attention. On top of that, it was a bit chilly. Anyway, I was bundled into a car and taken to a human house. It was all new. New smells. New noises. Green stuff everywhere (I found out later this was grass). I'll be honest, I was a little scared. Surrounded by all these unfamiliar sensations, I just wanted to curl up somewhere and hide.

Thankfully, the human female was kind to me. In the house, there was another human, a male human. He seemed nice, too. He seemed to spend most of his time in his chair looking at the paper.

I settled quickly in this new home. My humans were lovely but, if I am honest, a bit on the weak side. By that, I mean they let me do anything I wanted; there was no discipline. That's kind of hard for a dog, and it left me feeling that I had to take command. I'm not really a natural leader so am probably not that good at it. But, as these humans needed leadership, I had no choice. I have never seen a dog pack leader in action, so I kind of had to go by instinct.

First off, I decided that I had to bark at anything that came towards the house. If the intruder made a noise at the door, it was my job to warn them off. I did this by jumping up at the door and growling. My female human would take me aside and give me a tasty treat. That way, I learnt that jumping up at the door and barking at strangers got me excellent rewards. In fact, so rewarding was this that I took to looking out of the window and barking at anything that moved.

If a human was brought into the house, it was my job to jump up and down at them until my human gave me a tasty treat. I always got a treat, so I learnt that jumping up was a good thing to do. I also had to remind my humans that, when they sat down to eat, they had to give me some of their food. And there was no waiting – as alpha dog, I should be the first to eat. My humans turned out to be pretty smart and understood that really quickly. I always got something tasty from the table.

My humans also learnt quickly that I needed to be able to run around a lot every day. The sighthound part of me is quite strong and it meant that if I saw something like another dog or small furry animal, I felt an uncontrollable urge to go after it. I needed plenty of exercise, so I took these outdoor opportunities to chase anything I could see. I thought I was doing really well, but sometimes I could sense that the humans were not happy. However, this was of little concern to me.

Sometimes, my human would bark at me and run towards me. That was a great game. She never caught me till I wanted her to. The only problem with these excursions was that my human was too slow. I had to drag her along; otherwise, it would have taken too long to get to the park.

One thing I never understood is why my human

expected me to return if she stood there shouting "Kika" at me. I know she referred to me as "Kika", but why should I go back? I knew that if I went back to her, I would get a tasty treat. But didn't my human understand that there were sometimes more exciting things than treats?

Another part of my leadership duties was to remind everyone that I was boss. I did this by marking the house on a daily basis. My pet human kept trying to cover these marks with her own smell. Well, it wasn't her own smell; she would wipe the area leaving my smell overlaid with something that smelt lemony. I had to go and mark it again.

It was all a bit puzzling.

My human kept trying to teach me to do things like sit or lie down. I wasn't sure who was teaching who. I learnt pretty quickly that sitting got me a treat, so I started sitting to get treats when I felt like it. In fact, over time I taught my human to give me a treat whenever I wanted one, to give me food when I was hungry, to give me attention on demand and to move out of a chair if I wanted it. What I didn't like was when my human went out and left me. It happened from time to time, despite my best efforts to stop her. I even tried clinging to her all day, every day. But she didn't get the message.

Anyway, all this leadership responsibility had made me anxious. Nothing that bad, but I did feel uneasy a lot of the time. I was not even sure what I was anxious about. It was just very hard to relax with all these duties I had to carry out.

One day, my human bundled me into the car and took me on a long journey. Our destination was a small farm where I detected two other dogs – a small fluffy biscuit-coloured dog and a huge black and white dog. I was ready to bark at them, but I didn't get the chance. It was not my human that opened the car door but a male human I had never met before. I made to bolt out of the car, but I was blocked before I'd even got going. I tried again and again, but he just blocked me till I stopped. Then he put a lead on me, led me out of the car and made me sit. I tried some of my usual attention-seeking tricks, but he seemed indifferent to my demands and calmly, assertively, got me to do what he wanted. I had never met such a human before.

Sitting there, I looked around and saw that the other two dogs were also sitting. The big dog looked pretty excited and was making small whiney noises. The human made us all wait till we were calm before leading off on a walk. This tapped into a base instinct for us dogs – the pack walk – and in no time we had formed a small pack. We did this for a few minutes and then he took the big dog, George, and I into a field and let us run around. George was pretty playful and we had a great time.

When he took us back to the house, I realised that my human had gone and left me behind. It looked like I was going to be here for a while, so I decided to keep a journal.

This is that journal.

Day 1

At first, it felt a bit strange to be in this house without my human. The atmosphere felt different; I couldn't quite figure out what it was that made it feel this way. However, I did notice that I wasn't the centre of attention. As well as having two other dogs, the humans seemed to be always getting on with human stuff without involving me. I wasn't keen on this, so I started whining. This worked at home but, here, nothing! The humans just ignored me.

Eventually, I took my cue from the other dogs and retired to my bed. It's not that I desperately crave attention, but I had kind of got used to having my owner trained and ready to give me attention on demand. That said, if I am really honest, I probably do crave attention.

I didn't stay in my bed for long. I tried to get noticed by

just following the new humans everywhere. They still ignored me. They even moved me out of the way when I stood in front of them. They did this with their legs, so I couldn't count it as attention. Sometimes when I tried this "following the humans everywhere" strategy, the new human would wander over and pat one of the other dogs. That was really irritating. I tried butting in, but that didn't work. The humans just ignored me. I was puzzled; I just couldn't figure it out at all.

In the end, I found myself confined to my bed. I'm not sure how the humans did that, but once I was told to stay in my bed, I did. The funny thing was, I quite liked it. Blocked from my attention-seeking behaviours, I found myself just lying down and relaxing. That felt strange but good.

Dinner was a bit different too. We were all called into the kitchen and made to sit in a line. At first, I wasn't sure what was going on. I knew how to sit, though. Anyway, bowls of food were placed in front of us, and I got up to eat mine. I was intercepted by a sharp round sound from one of the humans and put back in my sit. The other two dogs hadn't moved. I got up again to eat my food. Once again, I found myself sitting. I looked at the humans and, although watching me closely, they seemed pretty chilled. That said, they were standing tall and strong. Something inside me shifted a little and I stayed sitting.

Then one of the humans made another noise, which sounded a bit like "OK", and the other two got up and started eating. So I did, too. I have to say, the meal was yummy and I wolfed it down so fast I hardly tasted it. With my bowl cleaned out, I headed over to help Maxi finish hers. I didn't get far before I was intercepted by the humans and sent away. That was a surprise. At home, I could do pretty much what I wanted. Here, I wasn't even allowed to share the other dogs' food. While I was disappointed, a tiny part of me felt content. I was part of a pack now, a pack I didn't have to lead. That was a bit of a relief really.

However, the behaviours I had learnt at home did not just stop there and then.

We went out later in the day. There was a big field here and we all went in, the three dogs and the two humans. George was a play dog, like me, so we were off having a great time. Then, two yappy little creatures came and barked at us through the fence. I wasn't having that, so I charged at them barking with all my might. The humans called me back, but I just ignored them, as I usually do. In fact, once I'd had enough of barking at the yappy dogs, I started running around the humans trying to get them to play.

They weren't interested, but that didn't stop me. I really wanted them to play. Ideally, we'd play catch where the humans tried to catch me. I'd let them get really close and then rush away. I could play that game for hours. However, the humans just walked over to the gate and out of the field. George and Maxi trotted out after them. Not me – I did my play bow and started charging around manically.

The male human returned a few minutes later and tried to catch me. *Great*, I thought, *I have got him playing at last*. He did manage to trap me, but only for a second before I wriggled free and shot off. It was great fun. Well, it was until the human shut the gate and disappeared leaving me on my own. I studied the gate but it was too high to jump over. There were gaps but they were too small to squeeze through. I did try to put my head through, but it got caught at a funny angle and I had to work it free again. As I couldn't get past the gate, I started chewing my way through. That worked because the male human came down. He called me, but I went into my play bow, charging around doing play bows and quick sprints. The human turned his back on me and put a steel barrier in front of the gate.

This barrier was a set of horizontal bars. I tried to squeeze my head through, but it wouldn't fit. I tried chewing it but got nowhere. After a while, I lost my play feeling and lay down. Eventually the human came to get me, and this time I followed him out and was taken back to the house.

I'd had a lot of fun, though.

Day 2

I worked out today that my new humans are called Adrian and Nicole.

We (dogs) had another quick run around before breakfast. Today I sat as instructed before wolfing mine down. I also managed to snatch some of Maxi's food before anyone could stop me. After that, I was confined to bed.

Thinking about it, I haven't really figured out George and Maxi. They seem to be quite independent dogs like me, yet they do what Adrian and Nicole tell them. George seems to like lazing around a lot. He also likes barking at visitors, just like me – maybe we can do that together. Maxi's quite different; she pretty much keeps to herself and does her own thing.

I got up to some mischief with my antics in the field again. I'm not sure why Adrian and Nicole think I should leave the field when they say so, especially when I am having so much fun. Today, I got the chance to bark at a human that was passing by. Again, Adrian and Nicole called me back, but I just ignored them. I know I get a treat if I go back when they call me, but barking at strangers is much more fun so there was no way I was going to stop. I was so focused on the stranger that I didn't see Adrian sneak up behind me until, all of a sudden, he had me by the collar. He put me on a lead, and I was on that lead for the rest of our time in the field and all the way back to the house.

Overall, there is more discipline in this pack than I have experienced before. The strange thing is, I kind of like it. I don't feel quite so anxious all the time. I have found that when I lie down and relax, Adrian and Nicole pay more attention to me, which makes it tempting to lie down and relax more.

Day 3

I am slowly getting used to life here but, today, Adrian and Nicole went out for a few minutes. While George and Maxi seemed quite happy with this, I was not. I was also puzzled when Adrian and Nicole returned because George and Maxi hardly reacted at all. I think Maxi got up and stretched her legs before lying down again. I jumped up and down and barked and barked. Despite all this action, Adrian and Nicole just ignored me. In fact, the other two dogs got attention, not me. I tried to butt in but was pushed away. Eventually, I gave up and lay down. Soon after that, I got some pats and strokes.

Since I've been here, I have noticed that if I persist with my jumping and barking, sometimes a loud bang comes from somewhere, startling me. I am never quite sure where this bang comes from. I suspect it's either Adrian or Nicole, but they never seem to hear it, let alone react to it. If it's not Adrian or Nicole, then dog logic dictates that it must be me that's causing the bang. My inclination to jump waned slightly.

Jumping and barking wasn't working, so I tried a different approach. When Nicole went out this morning, I copied the other dogs and did nothing. By that, I mean I just lay down next to George and dozed off. When she came back, I lifted my head but, otherwise, did nothing. I got a pat on the head. You know, it's a strange thing, but that different approach felt much less frenetic. Instead of worrying about Adrian's and Nicole's comings and goings, I just let them get on with it. I felt quite content.

However, things are not all plain sailing here. Instead of

playing in the field, we went on a walk around the village. By we, I mean Adrian, Nicole and we three dogs. We were all on leads – Nicole had George and Maxi, and I was with Adrian. As usual, I tried to run ahead of Adrian, expecting him to up his pace to match. That didn't happen. He just stopped and put me back next to his legs. He kept saying something that sounded like "heel". Well, I wasn't too impressed with this, so I just ignored him and shot ahead again. Adrian just stopped and pulled me back to where he wanted me.

I didn't like this at all. For a start, the others were getting ahead. Worse, they seemed not to care that I was falling behind. I pulled at the lead and started jumping up and down in frustration. I wanted to be at the front but here I was, being kept by Adrian's legs. I tried to everything I could to get free of the lead. Adrian just stood there, calmly ignoring me until I stopped. Then he put me down on my side. I struggled again, but he kept me there. Eventually, I wore myself out and submitted.

At that point, Adrian said my name and started walking. I was a bit tired now, so I just walked alongside him. After that, we caught up with the others (they had met someone and stopped to chat). The walk went quite smoothly after that. I was on a loose lead but if I tried to get ahead, I immediately found myself pulled back. In the end it was easier to trot along. Once again, a tiny part of me liked this. We were moving as a pack, with Adrian and Nicole leading, and I could just trundle along without having to worry about anything. Adrian and Nicole let us check out smells and p-mails, so it was all good really.

The behaviour of Adrian and Nicole was quite different to what I was used to. Nevertheless, I found it reassuring in a strange kind of way.

Day 4

It was just Adrian that took us on our morning walk today. We were heading for the field, and I was really excited about running around playing with George. I forgot I was on a lead and rushed towards the field. I came to an abrupt halt and in that moment, Adrian changed direction and I found myself behind him going in the wrong direction. I tried to pull towards the field, but he had a good grip of the lead so I had to follow.

I wasn't too keen on this, so I kept pulling away in the direction I wanted to go. Every time I got away from the heel position, Adrian changed direction. It was really annoying. After a while doing this, I forgot about the field and started watching Adrian. Almost by accident, I found myself trotting alongside him waiting for a change in direction. Sure enough, he did do a few more changes, but this time I was ready for him and followed smoothly. I was almost beginning to enjoy this. It didn't occur to me that this was exactly what Adrian wanted.

After we had walked around a bit, we went into the field gate. We all had to sit while the human took my lead off. I was the only one on a lead. I was desperate to get playing, but we were kept in our sit for a few seconds longer. At last, Adrian said, "OK," and we were off. Today, Adrian didn't call me back at any point. To be honest, I was having so much fun I'm not sure I'd have listened anyway. Perhaps Adrian was being smart. I mean, if I got away with ignoring a recall, then, using dog logic, I'd have learnt that it was OK to avoid recalls. That might be how I wanted things, but I'm not sure Adrian and Nicole felt the same way.

Things went well till Adrian decided it was time to go back. I didn't want to go back as I was having so much fun. So, when Adrian called us over to the gate, George and Maxi trotted over, but I stayed where I was. I found myself in a state of inner conflict. I really wanted to stay out and play with George. But George wasn't there anymore, so I was on my own. I could have gone over to the gate but, no, I wanted to carry on playing.

I dashed over near to where they were all waiting and did my play bow. I hoped George would respond and we'd carry on playing. However, without even looking at me, Adrian, George and Maxi went through the gate and left me on my own. That was perplexing. I didn't like being left on my own, but I also didn't want to go back. Adrian, George and Maxi disappeared indoors. Now, I wanted to go after them, so I started to chew the gate.

Again, that worked and Adrian came back out. I watched him approach. No George, but maybe Adrian would play with me, so I started dashing around the gate doing play bows. I reckoned that would get his attention but, no, he just ignored me and set up those same steel barriers to block my access to the gate. As they were made of steel (I later found out they were called sheep hurdles), I couldn't chew my way through them. Once again, I found myself on my own. I was there a while and, with no one to play with and nothing to do, I settled down to wait. Eventually, Adrian appeared and came down to the gate. I started my play bow routine again. Adrian just turned his back to me and looked like he was about to go back without me. Quickly, I trotted over and looked up. Before I knew it, I was on a lead and being led back into the house.

I was finding this way of life a bit confusing, so I decided to consult the other dogs. What I wanted to know was why they let Adrian and Nicole control things. Why do Adrian and Nicole decide when we go out, what we do, when we eat, when we do anything? I mean, George was a big dog – surely he could exert his authority? They both said much the same thing; they had both been through what I was going through. Both had tried to take control, tried to get Adrian and Nicole to do what they wanted. It never worked and, in the end, both had accepted this.

The thing is, and this is what I can't get my head around, they both said they were happier for it. "How could this be?" I asked. Again, Maxi and George were of the same opinion. "We have less to worry about," they said. "Plus, we like the structure, the discipline." I had to admit, a small part of me agreed with them. But I wasn't convinced. I went over and lay down in a corner to mull things over.

Later in the day, we went on a road trip. The three of us dogs were in the back of what Adrian and Nicole call a Land Rover. It wasn't sure about this so I started to whine. Nothing happened. I kept trying, but Adrian and Nicole just ignored me. In the end, I snuggled down next to George and, truth be told, it was quite a pleasant journey.

Day 6

The morning passed without much to report, but the afternoon walk was a bit of a palaver. It started in the kitchen where we dogs were put on leads. Nicole had George, and Maxi and I were with Adrian. The others went through the door and wandered off ahead. Adrian stepped through the door and beckoned me through. Then I was put in a sit. I couldn't contain myself. The others were getting ahead, so I charged off to catch up with them. I'd forgotten I was on a lead and didn't get very far. In fact, Adrian took me back inside and made me sit. I wasn't sure what to make of this and was a bit restless. Adrian just waited there calmly and patiently.

After a while, he went out and beckoned me through the door. Once more, I was put in a sit. Once more, I tried to run off after the others. Once more, I found myself back inside. We repeated this a few times until I did as I was told. Adrian locked up and off we went. I still wanted to catch up with the others, so I rushed ahead. Adrian just stopped, pulled me back next to his legs and made me sit. Again, this happened a few times until I gave in and trotted alongside him. It wasn't lost on me that we were making faster progress doing this his way. Once I had settled into the rhythm, I actually quite enjoyed trotting along.

We got to a field and I waited to be let off to play with George. Only, today, it didn't happen. In fact, George went off on his own to play with two other dogs. They were German shepherds and almost as big as George. It looked pretty rough. I was keen to join in, but remained in my sit and watched. I got some nice pats while I waited; I liked that. After a while, the two German shepherds left and we went for a walk up the road. We were all on leads and we all trotted along together. It was nice and I felt pretty good.

In the evening, some other humans came visiting. George barked, and I was straight up barking and heading to the door. I didn't get very far. The humans must have expected it because I was blocked straight away and sent back to my bed. All three of us dogs were kept in our beds. George and Maxi seemed quite content with this. I wasn't, but I was beginning to learn that it was better if I followed the lead of the other dogs. That said, Maxi wasn't as content as I first thought. As we lay in our beds observing the humans, Maxi started inching across the floor towards them. I watched with interest. She'd get about a dog's length along the floor before Adrian would get up, come over and gently hustle her back into her bed. If looks could kill – Maxi had quite an expressive face.

There was also food sitting on low-lying tables. At home, I'd have tried to help myself but here, I knew I wasn't allowed to touch it. What was unusual for me was that I didn't try. I was following George's lead, and he was just lying in his bed quite unconcerned about the food. I did the same and found that I, too, was quite happy there relaxing in my bed. I didn't have to worry about anything. At times during the evening, a human would come and pat us. We seemed to get more attention lying in our beds than

I did when I went around demanding it. It was a good reason to stay in bed.

Day 7

I had problems in the field again today. It was all fine; George and I were playing, and Maxi was mooching about doing her thing. She wasn't really a play dog. I think she was getting on a bit and just liked to wander around checking out smells. Anyway, I suddenly noticed that Adrian and Nicole had left the field and were at the main gate chatting to strangers. I didn't like that. I want it said that I am not a clingy dog – it's more that I can get a bit anxious if I don't have my humans close by. George and Maxi, as ever, seemed indifferent to the situation.

I charged over to the field gate, managed to break it and started to squeeze through. I was pretty pleased with myself. Before I got out, I found myself being pushed back and the gate was screened by the sheep hurdles. I reverted back to my play bow and dash routine. I wanted Adrian and Nicole in the field playing with me. I should have known by now that they would ignore me, which they did. With all my charging about, I didn't notice that Adrian and Nicole had come back and were leading Maxi and George to the gate. They were about to leave the field. I charged over to get George back before he escaped only to find a human hand grabbing me by the collar. Before I knew it, I was on a lead and sitting.

Later in the day, we went for a walk around the village. We were all on heel. This time, I did as I was told and walked to heel. The tiny part of me that likes all this started glowing inside me.

Day 8

I am aware that my behaviour is changing as I live here. I'm also aware that I feel a bit calmer in general too. I'm not sure if these two things are related. I am certainly learning that life is easier, and to some extent better, when I do as the humans ask. But old habits die hard. This is especially true when it comes to the field. When I get there, I go into a manic state with the determination to do what I want to do. All ideas about obeying the humans just go out of the window. This mirrors my behaviour at home when I am taken to the park, which is why it's an old habit and not something I have learnt here.

Today, as usual, I was left in the field with the gate blocked by the steel sheep hurdles. The difference was that, today, I found another gate, a big gate, and there was a bit of a gap under it. I managed to squeeze under the gate and run after the humans. I was not running after them to catch up, I was running after them as part of a game. Whenever the humans approached me, I'd do my play bow and then dash off in all directions. I felt I had the upper hand today. Yes, the garden, where we were, was still surrounded by fences, but I wasn't confined to the field. I felt free.

After one or two attempts to catch me, the humans disappeared inside. My nose was telling me that the other dogs were eating. Part of me wanted to join them, but the play part of me was stronger, so I kept up my dash and play bow even though no one was looking. Today, Nicole outsmarted me. I had to stop to go for a poo and while I was stationary, she caught me and put me on a lead. I spent the rest of the morning confined to my bed. I didn't mind that, as my bed was next to George and I liked lying near him. I felt inclined to follow George; he had a kind of calm disposition that inspired confidence.

But, as I said, my behaviour was changing. For one, I no longer felt compelled to follow the humans around the

118

house. I actually preferred lying in my bed. I wasn't barking at the door or jumping up on visitors, and I was learning to walk at heel. Not only learning, but also finding that I quite liked it – it's as though it gave me a sense of purpose.

Today, something new happened. After the afternoon walk, we got back to the garden. Normally we walk back to the house, although George and Maxi are allowed off lead. Today I, too, was allowed off lead. The human said, "Heel," and I trotted alongside him, as did George and Maxi. A part of me was really happy; I felt trusted. A bit of trust can go a long way with us dogs.

The evening, however, turned out to be a bit of a challenge. A human visitor came and I, for some reason, reverted to my old habits – I growled aggressively to see them off. As usual, I was blocked. Then I realised it was Matt. I loved Matt; he was often round at my nan's. I tried to rush over and jump up but was blocked. I had to wait in my bed. Blocked, as I was, I had little alternative than to wait, and then I calmed down and relaxed. That's when Matt came over to say hello.

This was a common theme here: I only got attention when I was relaxed. On the other hand, manic or aggressive behaviour was simply blocked or ignored.

Day 9

Author's note: Separation anxiety is a complex issue and can be triggered by many factors including the type of dog, the dog's nature and also the behaviour of humans. It is far too complex a subject to be covered in detail here.

Nevertheless, it is worth noting that dogs are pack animals. In the wild, a lone male wolf may leave the pack in search of a new pack. This would happen when it is not the alpha male but wants to be one. It's how wild animals spread their genes. Also, a wolf may wander off from the pack for some reason, but it will not lose contact with the pack. A wolf on its own is vulnerable.

It would be highly unusual for the alpha dogs to leave the pack. If they did so, it could trigger the pack into howling to call them back or even finding a new leader. If the humans are the pack leaders and they leave their dog behind, the dog may become stressed by this. This is quite understandable. In this scenario, a dog with separation anxiety might howl to call the humans back. Or it may become destructive. Or both. A good approach here is to wear the dog out before leaving so it's too tired to care. Having more than one dog can sometimes help.

If the humans are not the pack leaders, then the dog may also attempt to call the humans back. However, this situation is, from the dog's perspective, completely different insofar as the humans have left without its permission. In this case, this recall would tend to be an angry and persistent bark. An example of this is when a dog is left alone all day and barks non-stop.

It is my experience that humans tend to class both the above situations as "separation anxiety" and simply assume that the dog is miserable when being left alone. This can lead to what might best be described as prolonged goodbyes and/or enthusiastic return greetings – neither of which help the underlying problem. An excellent approach to separation anxiety is to play down the coming and going so that it becomes no more interesting to the dog than the human going into another room. On leaving and returning, the dog must be completely ignored as if nothing has happened, as if you have never been away. Humans find this very hard. It also only really works if the humans are the pack leaders.

The biggest challenge faced by dogs is the needy owner: the human that needs to say emotional goodbyes on the way out and then expect their dog to greet them with unlimited enthusiasm on their return. Good for the human. Disastrous for the dog.

I had a new experience today. Adrian and Nicole went out and left us dogs behind. As I have mentioned, I don't like being away from my humans and I hate it when I'm alone in the house. Yes, I had George and Maxi, but by alone I mean there were no humans. I suspect Adrian and Nicole knew I wouldn't like this as they had set up a dog crate for me. It was pretty comfortable. I have such a crate at home and feel safe when I'm in it. I was in my crate, and George and Maxi were stretched out on the floor nearby.

I howled with all my might.

Maxi and George were indifferent to my howls. The humans were elsewhere. Who was I howling at? I am not sure, but a dog howl is our way of calling the pack together. I wanted the humans back, so I was trying to call them back by howling. Eventually, they came back. I bounced around my crate hoping to be let out, but they ignored me. In fact, they behaved as though they had never been away. I couldn't understand why George and Maxi were not jumping up and down for joy. But they hardly moved. I was the only one doing anything.

I wore myself out pretty quickly and had to lie down. It was then that I was let out. Same old theme: I get what I want when I stop asking for it.

Day 10

It was a quiet day today. Adrian, Nicole and Matt sat around chatting. I had learnt that I got more attention when I just chilled in my bed, so that's what I did. In fact, today, it was Maxi that got into a bit of a pickle. She was trying to demand attention from the humans but, as with me, they just ignored her. It was good to see that the humans were consistent with all us dogs.

Instead of giving in and lying down (which I had learnt was the optimum strategy), Maxi started panting loudly and staring fixedly at the humans. It didn't change anything, but she persisted. It just goes to show, we dogs will be dogs. The humans have to be consistent with us every minute of every day; otherwise, our unwanted (by humans) behaviours can soon creep in again.

I am pleased to say that my decision to relax in my bed was rewarded with some quality pats.

Day 11

I am settling in here quite well. It's good having the other dogs around, and I am finding myself bonding with Nicole and Adrian. On top of that, George is a great role model; I find myself deferring to him more and more.

I am still finding my way with respect to the humans' rules; I get some things right and some things wrong. Luckily, Adrian and Nicole are quite patient with me, and I think I am learning. It's worth getting it right because as well as pats, I can sense a warm glow from Adrian and Nicole, and I like that. I must be getting somewhere because today I was allowed off lead in the garden area. It's a great place – there are trees to run around and a pond into which I splashed with an elegant jump. I love the water. The other two dogs seemed a bit reluctant to join me in the pond, though.

Matt went out on his own today. We dogs were made to sit in a line as he got into his van. It was hard; I could feel that all three of us really wanted to go and mob him. Maxi couldn't take it and broke away. George and I managed to stay put. Maxi nearly got run over because she ran under the van just as Matt was driving away. George and I watched all this unfold in a state of indifference. If we dogs could understand cause and effect, we'd probably realise that we had been put in a sit so as to avoid getting into danger like Maxi did. But we don't, so we just watched Matt's van disappear. Once we were let out of our sits, George and I had another play around the trees.

When we went back into the house, I was feeling pretty good – so good that I forgot myself and jumped up on the sofa. A loud bark and a stern look from Adrian and I was back on the floor in an instant. For some reason, Maxi snapped at me. I didn't react, but Maxi was confined to her bed straight away. I felt gratified, and my respect for Nicole and Adrian grew a little stronger.

Day 12

Maxi had a bit of a problem with her breakfast and brought it back up. I thought I might help myself, but Maxi was having none of it and warned me off with a growl before eating it herself. My status under threat, I started towards her, ready to attack and assert my dominance. I felt a hand grab my neck, and I looked up straight into Adrian's eyes as he said, "No!" He released my neck and pointed at my bed. I went scurrying out of the kitchen but stopped before reaching my bed. I was at a point on the floor where I had got used to marking my territory. I dropped my back legs and made ready to pee.

A loud clap startled me. I forgot about peeing and looked up. Adrian pointed at me and then moved his arm till he pointed at the door. Without time to think, I found myself scurrying to the door and I was let out. A clear message, indeed. If I was going to pee in the house, I would be sent outside. I wandered around the garden a bit, did my pee, went back and waited at the door. Soon after, Adrian let me in.

In that short exchange, Adrian had further asserted his dominance as pack leader. He had intervened to stop a fight and then given me clear instructions as to what I had to do. He had done it in a calm state without having to resort to violence or raising his voice. I have to say that I was impressed. I moved closer to accepting him as pack leader.

I looked around to see what the other dogs were doing. George was lying on the floor, one eye open, doing nothing but watching. Maxi was still trying to eat her breakfast. I then looked at Adrian, but he was doing human stuff and not paying any attention to us dogs. Same for Nicole. All was calm. I wandered over to my bed and lay down, watching. I felt calm also. I realised that I was not feeling anxious.

Soon after, Adrian and Nicole went out leaving us dogs behind with Matt. I began to feel anxious and started whining. Matt put me in the dog crate and also disappeared. That hadn't gone to plan! I sat there for a while not sure what to do before lying down and dozing off.

Day 13

I woke up in a funny mood and couldn't settle. It took a long time to get out to our morning walk. Every time I was put in a sit, I just got up again. I suppose I was trying to hurry things along, but I ended up slowing everyone down. Eventually, I did as I was told and off we headed. I was on the lead today.

I didn't learn my lesson because at the next walk, I carried on in the same way. This time, however, I found myself locked in my crate; and Nicole, George and Maxi went off without me. It was just me and Adrian. I carried on with my disruptive behaviour in the hope that I'd be freed and allowed to do as I please. This usually worked at home. Not here. Adrian just waited and read a book.

After a while, I gave up and lay down. This time, I found myself doing what I was told: sitting inside the crate, coming out when called, sitting outside the crate, sitting at the door before going out, sitting after going out and then walking to heel. We got out and started on the walk. We caught up with the others and, thankfully, I was let off lead so I could play with George. We had quite a long play session and I wore myself out. I was so tired that I walked to heel all the way back, did the sits when asked and then collapsed in my bed.

In the afternoon, there was something going on – it looked like Matt was leaving. I was too tired to care, but Maxi was obviously put out. She was doing her snail impression trying to crawl across the floor towards the humans. As ever, it didn't work.

After Matt had gone, we got to go on another walk. This time we went to the field where George plays with the two German shepherds. Today, they were there first and waiting for us. George was allowed off lead but Maxi and I were not. George took off and started playing with these large dogs. Part of me wanted to join in, but it was not to be. If I made any sign that I wanted to go and join in, Adrian blocked or distracted me.

When we got back, I had an unusual experience. I was still on the lead, but instead of walking back to the door, Adrian led me to a large plastic bin with wheels on. With me in heel position, he started pulling this bin along too. I was a bit startled and started jumping around trying to break free. Adrian just stopped, showed me the bin and then tried again. After a couple of false starts, I trotted along and realised the plastic bin was not a threat. Adrian seemed very pleased with me and I got some quality pats. I hope we do the bin again soon.

I have to say, I was as tired as I have ever been; and after dinner, I was fast asleep.

Author's note: You may be wondering why Kika was not allowed to join in the play with the two German shepherd dogs. The problem was that the German shepherds were dominant dogs, the female particularly so. Kika herself was not particularly well balanced. In this excited play state, allowing them to mix could have quickly gone wrong. The German shepherds' owner had no control over them and tended to shout their names at the top of his voice. The dogs' response to this was to get in an even more excitable state. In order to manage bringing Kika and the German shepherds together safely, I would have

125

needed to send the German shepherds' owner out of the field, and that was not something I was in a position to do.

Maxi was kept on a lead as she had a propensity to wander off. She got on fine with the German shepherds but was not interested in playing with them.

Days 14 & 15

The last two days have been quite quiet. Aside from our daily walks and games with George, not much has happened. The only real excitement has been the postman. When the postman comes, I do as I do at home: I bark manically and charge the door. Well, I try to but each time I am blocked. For one, the humans' body language makes it quite clear they own the door and that I come in at my peril. Also, the humans tell me to be quiet. They use a method we dogs use to keep puppies quiet during a hunt, so I know what they want. I just can't always do it and I find myself barking uncontrollably again.

When I bark after being told to be quiet, I soon find myself lying on my side with Adrian blocking any attempts to get up. I have to lie there till I relax. I can see that the humans are trying to teach me to be relaxed while the postman is there, but it's not easy. I have also noticed that this happens when I growl at things I detect going on outside near the house. That said, I am finding, more and more, that I am ignoring these outside activities.

The only other thing of note is that we were all given a bone to eat. What happened was that Adrian called the three of us over and made us sit in a line. I could smell something very enticing. Adrian reached over and his hand came back carrying a bowl. Six doggie eyes tracked every movement. As he placed bones in front of each of us, we strained to remain sitting. Eventually, Adrian said, "OK," and I snatched my bone. I love my food, so an extra bone between meals was just wonderful. I was the first to finish mine – no surprises there. Maxi wandered around the garden carrying hers. She had a look in her eyes that kind of warned you to keep away, so I did. George lay down and contemplated his. I did try to sneak in and take it, but George growled at me. I hastily backed away.

We dogs have our own code of discipline and, by now, I've accepted George as a high-status dog. I think he'd make a great pack leader – maybe better than the humans. His growl was a simple warning, and I accepted it. Anyway, George lost out in the end because one of the humans took his bone away. I did notice that he let them – no growling at the humans. That was a clear indication to me that George accepted the humans as pack leaders. Why? Because no self-respecting pack leader would ever let a lower-status dog take their food, even if they didn't really want it.

I was starting to get a clearer picture of my status here.

There was a big surprise in store, though. Maxi didn't eat her bone either and, to be honest, she seemed to be in a bit of a strop. One of the humans took her bone away, too. It was the same pattern as mealtimes: what we didn't eat was taken away. The humans controlled the food – another example of them enforcing their higher status.

Well, I'd had my bone and I was content just to lie there and chill a bit.

Day 18

It has been a few days since I wrote anything in my journal. I think that's a good sign. My basic needs of food and shelter and my breed needs of getting to run around are met every day. Boy, do I love to run. The difference between here and home is the structure and discipline. As a pack, we dogs need this; and I am finding more and more that I like the structure here. All in all, I feel quite settled.

I have also found that I am generally less anxious. I don't have to worry about lots of stuff. For example, at home there was always the chance of treats, so I was always on alert, just in case. Here, we get two meals a day and that's that. There are no snacks from the table. Instead of hanging around the table wondering if I'll get anything, I can just chill out in my bed – this makes life a bit easier. Talking of food, I have to admit that am pretty driven by food. Much more so than Maxi or George. So, while I can chill out and not worry about snacks from the table, I am nevertheless driven to find food in between meals.

Being quite young, there's still a lot of puppy in me, and I have been trying to use that to get more food. What I have been doing is wolfing down my meal as fast as I can and then trying to get food from George. It's what puppies do in the wild; in fact, it's where the jumping up behaviour comes from. We are jumping up at the mouths to get food. Because I was behaving like a puppy, I didn't get a telling off from George – he just turned his head away. The humans, however, got wise pretty quickly. I found today that after I had eaten breakfast, I was sent away from the food bowls by Adrian. I didn't have time to try my new trick. The same thing happened at dinner.

I have also noticed that George and Maxi never try to muscle in on each other's food. In fact, meal times are always pretty calm affairs. I suppose that's a good thing, in a way. But I would like more food. That said, I do get regular meals, so I can't really complain.

The other thing that happened today was that the humans went out and didn't lock me in my crate. I used my new-found freedom to jump on the couch to see where they had gone. The humans didn't see me, so I got away with it. This separation anxiety is a tricky thing. Neither George nor Maxi seemed to be affected; they just lay there and snoozed. They didn't go manic leaping on chairs or charging around rooms looking out of windows. I wore myself out, and then went and lay down next to George.

Day 21

Author's note: We were given strict instructions as to Kika's diet and how much to give her for her breakfast and dinner. What we were not told was the huge volume of snacks Kika was getting between meals. With us, there was only one intermeal snack each day: a treat after the main walk. It took till today for us to realise that Kika was not getting enough to eat.

I woke up hungry today. I know I talk about food a lot, but I seem to be constantly hungry here. At home, I got my meals but I also got lots of snacks in between. For example, my human would usually let me lick her plate clean. Here, I just get my meals plus the odd treat. I need more to eat, but all my strategies for getting extra food don't work here. This morning, I waited for my breakfast with my tummy rumbling. I was grateful to see that I had a bigger breakfast today. It even contained scraps of human food. I devoured it quickly as ever. Afterwards, I lay down with a full tummy and a contented look on my face.

Later in the morning, Nicole went to work. I just lay there and watched her go. Once she had gone, I dozed off. After our late afternoon run in the field, we were each given a bone as a treat. We were given these bones indoors, and Adrian made us stay in our beds until we had finished eating them. I had learnt from my previous experience of bones that both Maxi and George were slow to eat theirs. I also knew that George might block me from taking his and that Adrian and Nicole would block me from taking Maxi's.

Once I had finished mine, Adrian released me from staying in my bed. Despite all I had learnt, I couldn't help myself and ran straight over to Maxi's and George's beds to see if there was anything left. George, by this time, had

129

wandered over and collapsed on the rug. Sadly, Maxi and George had scoffed their bones, too. Feeling put out and wanting to make a point about my status, I went over and marked George's bed with a little wee.

Adrian saw this and took George's bed away, replacing it with a towel. I don't think George got my message. I found my liberty curtailed as I was confined to bed once more. I wasn't allowed out till dinner time. I had a bigger dinner than usual, and that was good. Today was a good day, food wise.

Day 23

I have been here for over three weeks now but, much as I like it here, I still struggle with not getting my own way. Before coming here, I could pretty much do as I pleased. Also, I could get my human to do things for me: food, attention, go outside, come back in, speed up on a walk – it was all within my power. Here, nothing happens when I try to get what I want. I don't even get negative attention like being told off. I just get ignored. I have also noticed that I like being around Adrian and Nicole when I am doing what they want. I know that they are pleased with me because I can read it in their body language. In a way, getting that subtle praise means I try harder to do what they want. These conflicting needs are hard to deal with.

I am an impulsive and impetuous dog and when I don't get what I want, I can't handle it. Today, for example, I was asked to sit at the front door. I wanted to go out straight away, but I was made to sit. I was so desperate to get my way that I sat, but I didn't sit still. I squirmed around and slid across the floor. I couldn't help it. I could sense something exciting was about to happen and I just lost control. All that happened was that Adrian closed the door, sat down on a chair and picked up a book. I sat and squirmed and slid and squirmed – all to no avail. Only when I sat still did Adrian get up, open the door and take me outside.

Over the last two days, we have been outside most of the time. Adrian and Nicole were doing something humans call "gardening". George and I were free to play as and when we wanted. I noticed for the first time that there were these large birds wandering around. The humans call them "chickens". I'm a sighthound – I see something, I go after it. It's in my breed. I ran after one. As soon as I started to chase it, I felt Adrian's hand on my collar and soon found myself tethered to a pole. That was a lesson I learnt quickly. Chasing chickens means I get tethered.

Yesterday, George played with the German shepherds again. I am still not allowed to, but I tried hard to join in. I was on the lead and I started whining, jumping around and generally carrying on. I pulled Adrian's arm in all directions, but he didn't seem to notice. In the end, I gave up and just walked along and watched. When we got back, George still had enough energy left to play with me, so that was good.

Today, I got a bit anxious when Nicole disappeared off. I stared out of the window for a long time, but she didn't come back. I gave up and lay down. I wanted attention, and my inability to get attention on demand still troubled me.

Day 24

I woke early and it was still dark. I wanted attention, desperately. I looked at George. He was stretched out as though he didn't have a care in the world, fast asleep. I looked for Maxi, but she had disappeared downstairs. All I could think about was attention. I had learnt that George, Maxi and I got attention when we were calm and relaxed. I had also learnt that demanding attention didn't work. But here I was, lying down, calm and relaxed, yet I wasn't getting any attention.

All of a sudden, I heard the humans' alarm clock which signified they were getting up. I leapt up and started running around in excitement. All I could think about was attention. Attention. Attention. Attention.

Of course, nothing happened; Adrian and Nicole didn't appear. I could hear them moving around, but they were in their bedroom and I was on the landing. It took them so long that by the time they appeared, I'd settled down again. That said, as soon as they appeared, I was up and jumping around them. I want attention. I want attention. I want attention. What did I get? Nothing! We went through the same routine of going through the door and down to the field. Actually, we had a good morning walk and a good breakfast. After breakfast, I tried to go and lie down in George's bed but was blocked by Adrian and diverted to my own bed.

We had extra walks and playtime today. By bedtime, George and I needed a good rest as we were both exhausted. I was so tired I forgot that I wanted attention. I fell asleep content with life.

Day 25

It rained a lot in the night; I could hear raindrops hammering on the roof. For some reason, Maxi was panting. She panted for what seemed like hours but nothing happened. I wasn't really sure what to think so I just ignored her. George did the same. It had occurred to me that Maxi might know something I didn't, something about rain, about how it might be threatening. George's calmness reassured me.

Part of my breed is Spanish water dog, so I am strongly drawn to water. With all that rain, I was looking forward to today. On our morning walk, there were puddles everywhere and everything looked really different. I loved it. I ran around and around, splashing through the puddles, having a brilliant time. Some of my sense of fun must have reached George and Maxi because they both joined in. We all got thoroughly soaked. When we went back to the house, I had a new experience. I got rubbed down with a towel. I loved that too. So did George. Maxi, though, looked a bit nonplussed. After that, we all had a good shake before lining up in our sits for our breakfast.

After breakfast, Nicole went out and Adrian disappeared upstairs. Although I feel less anxious these days, I still whined a bit, trying to call her back. As ever, nothing happened and eventually I went upstairs. Adrian was sitting in one of the rooms up there doing human stuff. From what I could see, he was looking at a screen and tapping on something with his fingers. I lay down on the landing nearby and dozed off. Whenever he moved, I leapt straight up. If he went downstairs, I followed right behind. He just ignored all this and carried on doing what he was doing. I ought to have known better by now, but I still felt this compulsion to be as close as possible to a human. My desire for attention was always there, just under the surface.

Today, the walks and play sessions went well. I had a lot of fun.

Later on, a stranger came to the door with a box. George usually barks when this happens, and so do I. Adrian and Nicole seem tolerant of this, but sometimes they ask us to be quiet. On this occasion, they were both upstairs so not in position to own or block the door (as they usually did). Adrian came down the stairs and barked, "Quiet!" George went quiet, sort of. He still did low, quiet occasional little barks. I just carried on barking while trying to get through the door. Adrian barked, "Quiet," at me. I ignored him.

Adrian flipped me on my back and planted his hand on my chest. He clamped my jaw shut, put his head next to mine and growled, "Quiet." I instinctively submitted and went quiet. I was learning that "quiet" really did mean I had to be quiet. I was also learning that barking at strangers was not something that got me rewards anymore.

Day 26

It was still pretty wet outside today and there were still puddles everywhere, so I made the most of that and splashed around to my heart's content. After we got back, I'd been towelled down and eaten breakfast, I was put in my crate. Soon after, Adrian and Nicole went out and left us. I was feeling pretty happy from my play session in the puddles, so I settled down and dozed off. I was still asleep when Adrian and Nicole got back. They opened the crate, but I was happy where I was and dozed off again.

In the afternoon, Nicole went out and Adrian was upstairs working on his computer. I lay in the hall outside his door. His door was open so I could keep an eye on him. At one point, he headed off downstairs. I followed and thought this would be a good opportunity to get some attention. While he was banging around in the kitchen, I sat in the middle of the floor and stared at him. I stared and stared and stared, but he didn't seem to notice. It was a bit disconcerting, but that was nothing compared to what happened next.

He went and patted George and Maxi. I was totally nonplussed. They weren't even demanding attention; they were fast asleep in their beds. How did they manage to get his attention by doing nothing while all my staring had failed? When Adrian disappeared upstairs again, I went and lay down on the floor near George. I was a bit miffed.

Day 28

Today marked me being here for four weeks. I like it here. I like the routine and I like being part of a larger pack. I also like not having to worry about a lot of things I used to worry about, like getting treats or having to bark at anyone approaching (although I still can't help myself sometimes), and so on. I have stopped marking the house now, as I no longer feel the need.

The one thing I am still struggling with, and I know I keep going on about it, is getting attention from Adrian and Nicole. It's funny when you think about it; you don't see us dogs going around demanding attention from each other. But we crave human attention. Well, I do. I have tried staring, following them everywhere, getting in the way, jumping up, jumping on the furniture, whining, howling and barking. I have even tried lying at their feet and doing my best to look adorable.

Nothing. I just get ignored.

I have even tried desperate manoeuvres like reaching around and trying to lick their hands as they put my lead on. Take today, for example. I wanted attention and had located Nicole in the kitchen. I sat in the middle of the floor and stared at her. I even shuffled my bottom a little. She just walked right past me and went upstairs. This was not what I wanted at all. I did learn, from this experience, that demanding attention can make the human go away.

I find it very hard not to behave in this needy, clingy fashion. I don't know if I have always been like this, but living at home with my mum has certainly strengthened this aspect of my behaviour. The problem is that old habits die hard. And today it was harder than ever because George had a slight injury to his foot, and Adrian and Nicole kept checking it. He loved the attention and stretched his leg out so they could get a good look. I could barely contain myself. I tried to butt in, but I just got sent away.

Later that day, Nicole came over to inspect George's leg. I tried pushing in, but I just got pushed away. I tried again, to no avail. I was so frustrated. Later again, I was lying in my bed with one eye open watching things. Nicole came over and gave me a pat. I was really happy. The thing I noticed was that neither George nor Maxi tried to muscle in. I was grateful, but I was also puzzled. Their behaviour was different from mine. As a rule, I felt inclined to follow George. Maybe I should I adopt his approach.

Aside from that, we had some good walks and some good play sessions. With his foot troubling him, George preferred to roll around on his back rather than run about. Still good fun, though. We had a heel walk this afternoon. I tried to get attention by not walking to heel. I got some attention insofar as I was corrected and put back into the heel position. Not really what I was hoping for – but attention is attention, isn't it?

We were in a different field today, and George and Maxi were allowed off lead, but I was still made to walk to heel. That was hard. I wanted to rush over and play, but we went round and round, changing direction, walking this way and that. If I moved out of heel position, Adrian would change direction and I'd find myself back in the heel position.

I did notice that if I walked in the heel position, I got some attention in the form of praise. Once I had realised this, I tried harder to stay in the heel position and, sure enough, I got more attention. Eventually, I was allowed off the lead and I headed off to play. We also spent some time in the garden. I was on a tether again, I think because the hens were out and about. I find them fascinating. The sighthound part of me felt instinctively compelled to chase them.

Luckily, George lay down next to me and we dozed off contentedly.

Day 29

George was not in the mood to play today. I tried to get him interested by charging around and doing play bows, like I usually do, but he just stood there and watched me. He seemed like he wanted to join in. He'd have a playful look on his face and would take a step towards me, but then he would stop. I was a bit puzzled; Adrian and Nicole weren't stopping him. With George behaving that way, I instinctively clicked into being pack leader.

Soon after, I heard strange people outside the house. They weren't too close, but they were close enough. I let off a menacing growl warning them to stay away. Nicole looked at me and told me in a stern voice to be quiet. I ignored her and growled again. At the same time, I looked straight into Nicole's eyes – I was challenging her. Well, she took me up on my challenge and I found myself on my back with her hand planted firmly on my chest. She growled at me and let me go. That was me told. I could still hear something going on outside but rather than growling, I looked at Nicole instead. She seemed disinterested in the noises, so I followed her lead and ignored them myself.

I could sense that Adrian and Nicole were getting ready to go out. Nicole went out most days, and sometimes Adrian went out at the same time. I didn't want to be left behind, so I did my best to point this out to them by getting in their way as much as I could. Dogs are very good at reading body language, so it was pretty simple to work out where Adrian and Nicole were heading, run ahead and sit in front of them. The net result of this was that I found myself locked in my crate. I watched with astonishment as they took George out, leaving me with Maxi. I couldn't remember George making any effort to get Adrian and Nicole to take him, yet there he was heading through the door while I was left behind.

Maxi and I were on our own. To be honest, I was too

astonished to whine or howl.

Later, they returned and I noticed George had something white wrapped around his leg. I heard Adrian and Nicole calling it a "bandage". George was also a bit dopey. He went straight to his bed and was asleep in an instant. I was let out of the crate and took the opportunity to try and get noticed. As you may have realised by now, my desire for attention and my strategies for getting it had been deeply ingrained into me. I did my best to get in my humans' way, time and time again.

Eventually, as usual, I found myself in my bed under strict instructions to stay there. I was still not sure how they did that, but there was something in their body language that touched some part of me. I stayed in my bed even though I could have easily just got up. I lay down, rested my head and followed Adrian's and Nicole's movements with my eyes. We were interrupted by Nicole giving us all a treat, some sort of chew. Quickly, I hid my chew in my bed and nabbed George's. I only got about two steps with it before Nicole had me by the collar and took it out of my mouth. I retired to my bed partly in surprise and partly in despair. Moments later, I settled down with my chew, George's chew now forgotten.

Nicole replaced George's chew next to him. Placed on the floor so close, George's chew now had my full attention. I waited a few seconds, checked that Adrian and Nicole were looking the other way and headed over to snatch it again. This time George growled. I froze. Adrian and Nicole had heard George's growl but instead of telling him off, I found myself locked in my crate. I didn't even have my chew. Taking George's food had led to me losing mine. That was a hard lesson to take.

George's chew was out of reach. Maxi's chew was out of reach. My chew was out of reach. There was not a lot I could do, so I gave up and settled down. Blocked from doing what I wanted, I found myself relaxing. I stopped worrying about chews and attention and all that. I then dozed off.

Day 30

I was up before Adrian and Nicole and thought it would be good to have a play with George in the house. He'd had a long sleep, so I was hoping his groggy state would have worn off by now. Adrian appeared and told me to go to my bed. I ignored him and carried on running up and down the stairs. My nails made a pleasing clacking sound on the wooden staircase. Adrian took hold of my collar, led me downstairs, put me in my crate and disappeared back upstairs. There was not much I could do, so I lay down and waited. At the usual time, we had our morning walk and play followed by breakfast.

Soon after breakfast, Nicole went out. George was sleeping next to Adrian's office. I lay at the end of the hall and watched George. He seemed content to leave Adrian to do his thing. He didn't demand attention once. The rest of the day was fairly quiet and I spent much of it snoozing. George was more into playing today, but was slowed down by the big sock he was wearing.

Day 31

Today, after our lunchtime walk, Adrian called us over and made us sit. I was first to sit and looked up expectantly, as I had learnt that this ritual usually led to a treat being handed out. Today we got chews. I had learnt that if I ate my chew and then went after George's or Maxi's chew, I'd be blocked. So, I dropped my chew, went over to Maxi and took her chew. I was just about to make off with it when I felt a hand on my collar. I dropped Maxi's chew and looked up in innocence. It was Adrian; he looked disappointed. He led me to my crate and locked me in. I had to lie there watching George and Maxi eat theirs.

A short time later I was released. However, instead of being left to my own devices, Adrian led me upstairs and made me lie down next to his office. I had to stay there for the rest of the afternoon while he worked. If he went downstairs for any reason, he would take me with him. It was pretty tiring; I felt I was working hard all that time.

After dinner, I was allowed to roam free once more. Adrian and Nicole were sitting on the couch, Maxi was in her bed and George was stretched out on the floor. I went over to George and nudged him with my nose. He didn't move – he just lay there ignoring me. We dogs don't play mind games. What you see is what you get. In that way, we are much like human infants. By ignoring me, George was sending a signal that, right now, as far as he was concerned, I didn't exist. While humans might struggle with ignoring one another, with dogs it's just something we do. By ignoring me, George was both exerting his status and telling me to go away.

Thinking about it, George ignored me a lot of the time now. He only really acknowledged me at playtimes. So, on the one side I had Adrian and Nicole watching me like a hawk, on the other, the dogs, George and Maxi, were ignoring me. The bottom line is that my behaviour (my usual tricks) was not working. I was not getting any reward from them. The kicker was that as well as getting no rewards from Adrian and Nicole, I was also alienating the other dogs.

In the dog world, dogs are not tolerant of unbalanced dogs. Some will try to snap us out of it. Others will simply ignore us. The natural conclusion was that George and Maxi sensed me as unbalanced. If this had happened in the wild, I could have been thrown out of the pack.

I was not sure what to make of this.

Day 32

I woke up at sunrise. With the sun rising earlier each day, it was pretty early, so the rest of the house was still asleep. Adrian and Nicole always got up at the same time irrespective of the sunrise. As I was awake, I got up and wandered around looking for something to do. George and Maxi left me to it. They were either ignoring me or still asleep. With nothing better to do, I did a poo on the floor. At home, that would have brought the human running – but here, nothing happened.

I lay down and waited, watching the bedroom door. Eventually, Adrian and Nicole got up and we went out for our morning walk. We went to the field where George and I had a good play, as we usually did. After breakfast, Nicole went out so the only human around was Adrian. Wherever he went, I was told to follow. Wherever he stopped, Adrian put me in the down position next to him. I found this quite tiring as it taxed my brain. Effectively, I was working constantly as well as battling the urge to get up and go. Strangely, part of me quite liked this routine. While it might seem quite restrictive, it was actually quite fulfilling. I had a purpose.

Our midday walk was around the fields, and George and I ran ourselves into the ground. We were both worn out. I am lucky that I have George here. I am a young dog with boundless energy, so need these play sessions to wear myself out. I love them. When we got back, Adrian had treats ready for each of us. It was a chew. We were lined up and put in a sit. I broke mine in an attempt to get my chew more quickly. I was put back into my sit in exactly the same position. Once we were all sitting still, Adrian handed a chew to each of us, George first, then Maxi and me last.

I headed over to my bed to eat my chew. As I settled, I couldn't help noticing that Maxi had left hers behind. She didn't want it. I was tempted, but I could feel Adrian's eyes watching me, so I stayed put. Adrian picked up Maxi's chew and dropped it next to my bed. George was in his bed next to mine, and I noticed he was looking at Maxi's chew with interest. Maxi had wandered off. I waited. I could feel Adrian's watchful gaze. More than that, his body language clearly told me that it was his chew. He owned it. That was a simple message for a dog. We know instinctively that to move for a higher-status dog's food could be a bad move. I lay there watching Adrian, my eyes occasionally flicking towards the chew. George also lay motionless. We both tracked Adrian's movements, waiting for a sign that we could take the chew.

Eventually, Adrian picked up the chew and wandered off. His body language radiated satisfaction. I felt like I had passed some sort of test. George and I got on with chewing our chews.

Next up, Adrian gave us the command to stay in our beds, and then he wandered through to the kitchen. I got up and went to see what he was doing. I was still thinking about Maxi's chew. I kind of hid from view hoping he wouldn't see me, but he did. I was sent back to bed with a growl ringing in my ears. I stayed put this time.

We went for another walk in the afternoon where George and I ran and ran and ran until we both had to stop. We walked to heel on the way back, too tired to do anything else. Once home, I was glad to be able to lie in my bed and rest. At dinner time, I noticed that I wasn't being watched, so took the opportunity to jump up at George's mouth hoping he'd give me some of his dinner. Turns out I was being watched and found myself in my bed straight away. I gave up, relaxed and dozed off.

Day 34

I woke up again early today, but this time I stayed where I

was and waited. I had learnt that there was not much point in getting up before everyone else. Besides, we have a morning play walk every day so I knew I'd be getting out soon. It was very cold and frosty when we did go out and the ground was quite hard. I'm not sure why but we dogs do love a cold and frosty morning. Nicole was with us this morning as Adrian had gone off somewhere on his bike. George and I tore around having the time of our lives.

While playing, I spotted a strange man approaching and went berserk. Even when I realised it was Adrian returning, I carried on barking. He gave me a look which caused my barking to falter. I turned and trotted over to Nicole where I sat down. Nothing happened, so I ran off after George.

I don't normally remark on our meals because they are always pretty good, but today we had warm gravy on our breakfast. I loved it, but Maxi brought hers up all over the floor. I stared at it really wanting to go and eat it up myself, but, as ever, I was blocked before I even moved. I wondered if Maxi sensed my interest because she ate it up herself pretty quickly.

I was finished first so first into the lounge. I waited wondering if I would get any leftovers from the other dogs' breakfasts. It had never happened before, but that didn't mean I had lost hope; well, not yet anyway. Sometimes, like this morning, I got a bit overexcited, and today I greeted George when he came into the lounge as if I hadn't seen him for ages. Nicole came over and sent me to my bed. I lay down, relaxed and stopped worrying about food.

Even though it was cold, we spent a lot of the day outside in the garden. The hens were out, so I was restrained. By that I mean I was on a lead. Adrian and Nicole don't trust me around the chickens. In the afternoon, George and I had a long play session. I think the frosty air encouraged us to play longer and harder than usual. After that, we both slept right through to the next day, getting up only for our dinner and evening walk.

Day 35

After breakfast today, we could tell that Adrian and Nicole were up to something. We didn't know what, but all three of us dogs were watching them with our full attention. We wanted to be involved. We certainly didn't want to be left out. We were ecstatic when Adrian and Nicole got our leads and called us to the door. I was ever so excited. Too excited, as it turns out, as I couldn't walk to heel. I kept trying to charge ahead. Each time I lunged forward, Adrian would execute a 90 degree turn to the left or right and I'd end up careering into his leg. We did quite a few of these turns before I calmed down and walked to heel.

Eventually, we got to the gate where Nicole, George and Maxi were waiting for me. We were taken down to one of the fields we often go to. Adrian and Nicole were carrying some gardening tools and a bunch of sticks. When we got to the field, Maxi and I were put on leads attached to posts. I was not happy about that, so I started whining and carrying on. Adrian and Nicole just ignored me and started putting the sticks in the ground. I didn't give up; I still expected my whining to get me somewhere as it always had in the past. Not today.

Maxi lay down and went to sleep while George wandered around doing his own thing. I tried to attract George over with a bit of body shimmering, but he wasn't interested. I went back to whining. After a while, I stopped whining and lay down. I was wearing myself out. Soon after, Nicole came over, took me and George into the field next door and let us play for a while. That was great. After we'd had a good run around, I was taken back to my tether and Nicole carried on planting sticks. I whined again, but not as long this time. I lay down and watched. Soon after, I got to run around with George for a while.

A pattern was emerging. If I whined and carried on, I got nothing. If I was quiet and relaxed, I got to play with

George, plus I got some human attention. Another cog clicked deep in my mind.

At one point Nicole disappeared off for a while leaving us with Adrian. He was still planting sticks. When she came back, Nicole had some treats for us dogs. Bones – yum! As usual, we had to sit for our treats. I managed it today and lay down happily to eat my bone. Maxi was not that interested in her bone. I am always a bit puzzled by this; Maxi never seems that interested in bones or chews. I kept one eye on hers with a view to stealing it. However, I was aware that Adrian and Nicole were watching me, so I let it be.

We were out all day. Adrian and Nicole must have planted a lot of sticks. We headed back just before it got dark. George and I were allowed one more play before we went inside. I never tire of these play sessions; they're great and it means I get plenty of exercise. After dinner, I went straight to my bed. I was exhausted. No hanging around waiting for the others. No watching Maxi's or George's food hoping for treats. I just headed over to my bed and flopped down. I had come to really like my bed. I always felt pretty relaxed when I lay in it, and I really liked feeling relaxed.

Day 36

Today was much like yesterday – more stick planting. I was more relaxed today, and I lay down watching but not whining. Adrian or Nicole let George and I play from time to time. When we got back, late afternoon, I lay down in my bed for a welcome snooze.

When Adrian started putting together our dinner, the smell hit me head-on. I was back on alert. Food was in the offing. Here, we dogs were not allowed in the kitchen while our meals were being prepared. Back home, I'd be under my mum's feet the whole time. Sitting in my bed while dinner was being prepared was very hard for me. On top of that, Adrian and Nicole had a habit of calling us over for dinner one at a time. I think they called this "working for our dinner". I knew the body language that signified we were about to be called. No sooner had I spotted Adrian getting ready to signal us, I shot across the floor.

I careered into his legs, which he had planted in my way. Adrian raised an imperious arm and pointed to my bed. Reluctantly, I slunk back. Tonight, Maxi was called first. No sooner had the syllable "Ma" come from Adrian, I immediately darted across the floor. Once again, I careered into Adrian's legs and was promptly sent back with a stern command. This happened again. Eventually I waited, and Maxi and George were called for their dinner. Then, they were allowed to eat, but I was still in my bed.

Adrian came over and told me to sit. I couldn't sit still and squirmed all over the place. Adrian turned his back on me, went and sat down and picked up a book. I carried on squirming and carrying on. Nothing. Adrian just ignored me and read his book. After a while, I stopped squirming and sat there motionless, eyes fixed on Adrian. I knew that Adrian was likely to ask me to sit, so I pre-empted him. Adrian looked across at me and started to stand up. I started squirming with excitement. Adrian collapsed back into the chair with a sigh and went back to his book.

This cycle was repeated quite a few times. Eventually, Adrian manhandled me into a sit and froze me with a look. I sat still. After a few seconds, I was heel-walked over to my dinner bowl. I again had to sit. I sat still; I was allowed to eat.

Later, at the evening walk, I couldn't sit still at the door. Nicole took Maxi and George out, leaving me with Adrian. He fixed me with a stare, so I sat still. We went through the door and Adrian told me to sit. I sat, but I wanted to catch up with the others. I knew I'd be back through the door if I stood up, so I started squirming instead. Adrian took me back through the door into the kitchen and fixed me with a stare. He just stood there all calm and relaxed, waiting till I did as I was told. Eventually, I managed to sit still both sides of the door and we went over to join the others.

Day 37

One challenge we all face, dogs and humans, is when we dogs get fixated on something. When that happens to me, I can be vaguely aware that Adrian and Nicole are calling me, but I just tune them out. What I am doing is just more interesting or rewarding. This can vary from breed to breed, but with me it's barking at strangers and, to a lesser extent, hunting. If I see a stranger near my patch, I want to bark and growl at them to warn them off. I am much like George in that respect. The difference is that when this happens, George responds to the human calls, whereas I ignore them.

For example, today, I saw a strange human in a nearby field and barked. George joined in. Adrian and Nicole told us to be quiet. George turned away from the stranger and wandered back to Adrian and Nicole. I carried on barking and growling menacingly. Even though I know I am not doing what I'm told, I can't help it. It doesn't happen that often, as Adrian and Nicole are pretty alert; and if they see something before I do, they move quickly to block and distract me. I get rewarded with attention for being tolerant of strangers. I get forced to submit if I am disobedient.

Through this consistent approach, I can feel myself changing, albeit slowly. Truth be told, it's quite nice not having to worry about strangers and to know that Adrian and Nicole have it all under control. That means more time for play and sniffing p-mails. What's interesting, though, is that George doesn't always respond to Adrian and Nicole in

147

these situations. Someone had left the gate open and George, on seeing a passer-by, shot out, barking like mad. He ignored the recall till he'd finished, at which point he trotted back looking very pleased with himself. Maxi even joined in on that one. I missed out – I was on a lead.

It's also interesting that we dogs never get punished for these lapses. Adrian and Nicole seem to understand that we dogs don't really understand cause and effect. We have to be intercepted in the moment; otherwise, we just get confused. For example, if George had been punished for his barking charge when he got back, he would likely have interpreted that as being punished for coming back. It goes to show, we dogs need informed, constant and consistent behaviour from our humans, or it's all too easy to develop what humans might call "bad behaviours".

Day 38

Following on from yesterday's musings, today was a case in point. We were about to go through the gate into the field to play. I was pretty excited, but I was sitting, waiting, like George and Maxi, while the human dealt with the gate. I heard some human voices nearby and let off a menacing growl. I was given the "quiet" command, but I continued to growl. As I was mid-growl, I found myself flipped on my back with a hand placed on my chest. That stopped me. I didn't struggle; I just lay there. I noticed that, as I lay there, if I did nothing, I got some attention including a bit of a pat. If I growled, I got a sharp nudge to snap me out of it.

Had I been able to think like a human, I might have wondered what life would have been like had my mum been a bit more aware. I think her problem was that she liked all my excitable behaviour; it served her needs as a human. My needs as a dog came a poor second. The more I got rewarded for being aggressive and excitable, the more I developed those behaviours in order to get more rewards. In essence, this is one of the reasons I growled at the human voices I'd heard – I had learnt that growling in such situations got me rewards. Once we dogs have learnt a behaviour that gets us rewards, it's not easy to unlearn it.

Later in the day, we had a brilliant play session. If I ever go back home, I'll miss these playtimes. I have grown quite attached to George. I feel happy to cede to his higher status and I think, in an odd way, that has helped me, over time, to accept Adrian and Nicole as pack leaders.

Day 42

Today I could tell something was up straight away. Adrian's and Nicole's body language were different. They were planning something. All three of us dogs watched them closely. The hint of excitement in the air was infectious. Of course, Adrian and Nicole made us wait in the lounge while they got their human stuff ready. It was hard, but not as hard as it used to be. Finally, we were all put on leads, taken out and put in the car.

It wasn't a long drive and we had hardly settled before the back of the car was opened. Getting out of the car was, as usual, a strictly controlled process. We all had to sit in the car and wait. One by one our leads were put on and we were allowed to jump out. Then we had to sit again. I could hear and smell a lot of dogs. George seemed pretty excited. That was unusual. I wasn't too sure – this was new and, well, all those dogs. Would it be OK? I was a bit scared if I'm honest. Maxi seemed totally indifferent.

Once we were all ready, we were walked on heel through some gates. We were now closer to the other dogs, and I could see some looking at us through a gate. George was really excited now, but I was still a bit scared. We had little time to react before George and I were passed to another human who headed off with us. He didn't seem to be too bothered about heel walking; he just walked quite quickly. We were in the field and all these dogs were coming over to sniff us. With no ceremony at all, George and I were let off lead. George was straight off and, in a flash, he was playing. I followed him. I did try to nip a couple of dogs that got too close but, to be honest, I just got caught up in the moment.

The energy was playful, not threatening, and my anxiety evaporated as I ran flat out with the new dogs. In fact, I started to have such a good time that I didn't even notice my humans disappearing. We were taken indoors later in the day and put into kennels. We had our own beds; we recognised the smell. We were also given our dinner. To be honest, I was almost too tired to eat. George and I were completely worn out; we had run ourselves into the ground. I hardly even noticed that my humans were not here.

It had been a good day.

Day 43

This morning I woke up in a new place. George, Maxi and I had shared a kennel. I was more than happy with that, though I'm not sure Maxi was too impressed. We didn't go out with the other dogs; instead, we were taken to an area for just the three of us. Soon after, a gate opened and Nicole and Adrian came in. I ran over full pelt with a mind to jump up. I didn't get the chance as I was expertly caught, put into a sit and had my lead fitted. Then we were bundled into the car. I say bundled, but it was quite orderly really, one at a time with the usual sits before and after.

Soon we were back home. I say home because I was beginning to feel like this place was my home now. I'd been here for six weeks – a long time in any dog's life. George was a bit off his food today and didn't eat his breakfast.

Despite all my training here, I went for it. As ever, Adrian and Nicole had anticipated my actions and I was blocked. To be honest, we were all still pretty tired from yesterday, so we all went to our beds and passed out.

The rest of the day was back to normal. Although I have to admit that George and I didn't play as much – too worn out from yesterday.

Days 44 to 47

The last few days have passed in a bit of a blur. After our short stay at the place with all the dogs, our routine carried on as normal here. I'd love to say my behaviour has been exemplary, but old habits die hard. I get things right a lot of the time, but not always. Food and attention-seeking remained at the root of many of the problems.

George and Maxi get it right pretty much every time. Me, most of the time, but not always. The hardest time for me is just before breakfast. I know that after we get back from the morning walk, we have breakfast. This means I am prone to trying to get through the door as quickly as possible. A couple of days ago, I rushed through the door and tried to pull the human with me. I found myself outside again. I had to sit while Maxi and George were given their breakfast, and then I was led off on a short heel walk. At first I protested, but I soon gave in and walked to heel. Only after that did we go back to the door. This time I followed instructions and got my breakfast soon after.

I've got better with the postie, though. Yesterday, I think, the postie came up, opened the door and dropped a parcel into the kitchen. I didn't bark or growl. Adrian and Nicole noticed this, and I got some praise. I liked that.

Last night we had some visitors, and that caused me to bark. Although I did bark once or twice after being told to be quiet, I calmed down pretty quickly. As ever, when I was calm and lying down, Adrian and Nicole came over and gave me some attention. That was great. Not much else to write about really. George and I had our energy back and we had some good plays. All in all, the last few days have been pretty settled.

Day 48 – Home Again

There was something up today. Adrian's and Nicole's body language were borderline excitable. The mood was infectious and I felt myself getting all excited too. Normally, at this time, Nicole would be heading out and Adrian would be going upstairs. Today they seemed busier, excited, and they were packing bags. We three dogs tracked their every move. I hoped we were going to be a part of this, whatever it was, and not be left behind on our own. The usual rules applied, so we watched the human activity from the lounge. They did not like us getting in the way, much as I liked to.

At last, we were called into the kitchen and lined up by the door. *Great*, I thought, *we're going, too.* We were taken out and put into the car. George and I were pretty excited. Maxi was not; she doesn't seem to like car journeys. I paid her no attention.

It was a long drive today. After our initial excitement, we soon got bored, settled down and fell asleep. From time to time, George or I would wake up and look out of the windows. There was not much to look at, just trees passing by. After what seemed like an age, we stopped and the car engine was turned off. George and I sprang up and looked through the window. Maxi was still sitting there, in the corner. I'm not sure that she had moved since we set off.

I looked out of the window again. This place seemed familiar. The back of the car opened and we sat waiting for our leads to be put on. Once out, we had our leads attached and then we set off on a walk. Something about this place smelt familiar; I was pretty sure I had been here before. I wanted to explore further but being on a lead stopped me. There were other humans and dogs around, which both George and I watched with interest. As ever, at the slightest hint, our interest was turning into fixation. A quick nudge from a human distracted us.

It was not a long walk and we soon found ourselves back in the car. If I were a human, I might have wondered why we had come so far for such a short walk. As a dog, I just enjoyed the moment. This next drive was much shorter and before we'd even had a chance to doze off, we were parked up again. Like jack-in-the-boxes, George and I sprang up to take a look. I recognised this place too; it smelt familiar. Realisation dawned – it was my home. I had not seen it for nearly seven weeks, but it's not a place I'd forget. I was suddenly so excited I couldn't contain myself.

We had to go through the usual ritual when getting out of the car. How I managed it the first time I just don't know. Once we had all disembarked and lined up in our sits, we were taken to the door. The door opened and out came my mum. I could tell she was really pleased to see me. I might have charged over and jumped up, but Adrian had control of the whole situation. I was allowed to approach my mum, but there was no jumping up. Also, I only got a cursory pat. I think Adrian was keeping my mum under control too. I don't know how he managed that.

Anyway, we dogs were led into the house. My dad was there sitting in his favourite chair. He just gave us a wee wave but didn't get up. George and I were led to our beds and placed in a down. To be honest, I was pretty tired from the long car trip, so I was quite happy. It was interesting reading Adrian's and Nicole's body language. Unlike my mum and dad, Adrian and Nicole were quite chilled, almost as though this was just another normal day.

My dad had seemed quite tense when we three dogs appeared in his living room. My mum seemed a bit put out.

Maybe she was hoping for a more excitable greeting from me. But I was done with that; this chilled approach was much more to my taste. The atmosphere in my house was good and calm. George and I settled down and dozed off. That seemed to relax my dad. We got a lot of attention, though, with humans coming over and giving us pats and praise. I drank it up.

Maxi was allowed to wander freely. She didn't seem to know what to do with herself and wore herself out trotting around checking everything. Of course, she used to live here, too. After a while, George, Maxi, Nicole and Adrian left, and it was just me with my mum and dad again.

On Reflection

I am writing this having been back home for a wee while now. I know us dogs live in the moment, but I feel I need to reflect a little on what happened. Please bear with me as I try to translate my doggie thoughts into human-speak.

Looking back, I can see that when I was dropped off at Nicole and Adrian's place, I was not a balanced dog. I had learnt all sorts of behaviours that had turned me into something of an anxious dog. Living with Nicole and Adrian had helped undo much of that, and I felt a lot better for it. It had also helped having George there. He was as laid back a dog as I have ever met; he had a strong influence on me.

In human terms, my mum had treated me a bit like a human princess. She had pandered to me and indulged my every whim. I suspect she thought that treating me like a human child would make me happy. The reality was that she enjoyed indulging me because I think she liked to do so. While I enjoyed being indulged, it also caused me to become unbalanced.

We dogs, we need exercise and discipline. Affection is

important, but comes a distant third in our needs. I had tons of affection, enough exercise and no discipline – this had turned me into a needy, bossy dog. I barked at visitors, attacked the postie, growled at passers-by, jumped up and demanded food and attention at my convenience. I never really felt settled. I was always anxious. I would whine for hours if my mum went out. I was even sent home from a dog day-care centre for being too clingy. Not a good picture however you look at it. Yet, my mum seemed to like my clingy and excitable behaviour and, through her actions, she re-enforced my anxiety and "bad" behaviours.

Much of what I have written in my diary is about the times where my behaviour did not get me what I wanted. Quite the opposite, in fact. Humans translate this into human-speak as "bad behaviour", but to me it's just what I have been trained to do by my mum.

For example, treats. I admit I am quite an excitable dog at the best of times. If I think a treat might be forthcoming, I am instantly excited. This means I get all animated and pushy. I try to lick the human's hands or jump up or just generally get in the way. Or all three of the above. If I behave like this around my mum, I get both the treat and lots of attention. Even better, if I feel like a treat, all I need to do is act excitable around my mum and she gives me a pat, a treat and tells me I'm a good dog. At Adrian and Nicole's, it was the opposite. If I acted all excitable and demanding, I got nothing. I only got a treat once I had sat still (on command) or when I was receiving training.

During my time at Adrian and Nicole's, I felt my behaviour change. Mainly, I found I spent more time relaxing and less time worrying about getting attention and treats. I still fell back into my old habits a lot of the time, but I think that's understandable. It takes time for new behaviours to kick in. It takes even longer for new behaviours to become the "default setting". The thing is, all in all, I returned home a happier dog. Being able to relax means I have a better quality of life generally. I mean, if you think about it, you don't see wolves all charging around trying to get attention from each other. Wolves hunt, eat, rest and sleep. When not hunting, they like to just chill out and watch the world go by. I think what I am trying to say is that, at Adrian and Nicole's, I felt more in touch with my inner wolf, and that felt good.

During my time at Nicole and Adrian's, I learnt about discipline. I am talking about dog discipline, not human discipline. For dogs, discipline just means a set of rules by which the pack lives. As a pack animal, it helps us maintain a balanced pack. It is what stops us ripping each other apart. I think humans sometimes confuse discipline and punishment. Big mistake when it comes to dogs.

I grew to love those rules, even if I sometimes forgot them and broke them. I felt more like a complete dog rather than a human plaything. Nicole and Adrian had also done some training with me. This was mostly recall. I am not quite sure how they did it, but when called, I came back whatever I was doing. It was as if I had no control over my muscles. I heard the recall command, and I was on my way back before it had even registered in my brain.

It saved my life.

A few days after my return, I was on a walk with my mum and I saw a deer. It ran and I was straight after it. It was heading for a busy road, but this didn't register with me. All I could see was the deer. As a sighthound, the thrill of the chase is deep-rooted in my breed. Nothing could stop me in full flight. If that deer headed across the road, I'd be right behind it, cars or no cars. I heard my mum shouting out the recall command and, before I knew it, I had skidded to a stop, executed a U-turn and was haring back to my mum. She seemed really pleased, and I got loads of pats.

I'm not sure my mum really learnt from that experience, though. My feeling is that I have changed a lot, but my mum is just the same as she ever was. I love her to bits, but I can't respect her. I think the big difference between here and Nicole and Adrian's place is that Nicole and Adrian met my needs as a dog. They saw me as a dog and had a set-up in place which met all the needs of us dogs. Nicole and Adrian were strong and fair leaders. I respected them. Here, I think my mum puts her needs first. She likes to have an animal that runs around doting on her. It's not good for me, but I don't think she can see it. It is a lot of pressure to put on a dog when you think about it.

Much as I hate to admit it, since I have been home, I have regressed a little. I jump up at visitors, growl and bark at passers-by and sit staring at the dinner table till I get my snack. I get lots of attention and treats, but the result is that I have gone back to feeling anxious a lot of the time. When it comes to recall, I do return when called, but not every time. Sometimes, I am too engrossed in what I am doing.

I have overhead my mum calling Adrian on the phone to discuss some of the more aggressive aspects of my behaviour, but I am not sure what these calls have achieved. From my perspective, not much seems to change.

Nevertheless, as I have got older, I have calmed down a lot and have also learnt a bit more about humans. I would best describe my current life as one where my mum and I have reached a kind of "understanding" in which I indulge her. This is not easy for me insofar as there is a lot of pressure on me to meet my mum's needs, and I am not really well equipped to do that. But, overall, I think I am OK.

Haribo

Haribo

My name is Haribo and I am a tricolour collie. When this book was first mooted, I was not keen to tell my story. I don't seek the limelight. All I really want to do is play ball, lie in my bed and have two square meals a day. Beyond that, I am not interested in much else except pats. I am quite different from the other dogs featured in this book. Collies are bred as herding dogs, and this means we have to be in constant communication with our human. Our human tells us where we need to be, what position to adopt, and so on, so the sheep can be successfully herded. That means it's in my nature to seek instructions from a human. I am not independent like the other three.

Because I am inclined to do what I am told, my story is much shorter, and I was a bit worried that it would make me seem less interesting. I have been assured that this is not the case and that all dogs are equal. Truth be told, we are all treated the same, so that rings true.

Eventually, after much persuasion, here is my story.

In the first two years of my life, I've had five human homes. The first returned me to my birthplace after only a few weeks. My fifth owners were a human couple but, one day, I was passed to my man-human's mother. She already had a dog, a Labrador called Bounce, and I never felt welcome there.

We (myself and Bounce) used to be left at a dog day centre, DogiPlayce, two or three times a week. I didn't really like DogiPlayce as I had to wear a muzzle. There were also too many dogs, and I was not keen on strange dogs. In fact, I really didn't like them at all, and was prone to make sure they knew this by charging at them biting and growling. I was also quite possessive, so I didn't like it when Bounce got attention. He used to play a lot with a large black and white dog called George. I used to butt in to try and stop Bounce. It didn't really work. George and Bounce

160

just ignored me and carried on regardless.

The rest of the time, I would sit at the edge somewhere and watch hoping I might get to play ball.

One day, I was taken to DogiPlayce on my own, without Bounce. I looked everywhere, but Bounce was nowhere to be seen. I had been left there on my own. I think my new owner had gone on holiday and taken Bounce but not me. There is only so much rejection any creature can take. I found a corner, lay down and made myself small.

I noticed that, on my first day at DogiPlayce on my own, the DogiPlayce staff were looking at me more than they usually did. There was one human who was often in the field with us dogs. He had pretty good control over us given there were sometimes around 50 dogs charging about. He was always on top of things and stopped aggression and games getting out of hand. Sometimes he'd play ball and I'd join in. There were a lot of dogs chasing the ball, so he used to throw lots of balls in different directions to spread us around and keep us moving.

That day, he was looking at me and talking to the DogiPlayce staff. I ignored them. Next day, a female human came and looked at me. She tried to tempt me over for some pats, but I wasn't interested. I just wanted to be left alone.

New Home

A few days later, the male human I mentioned earlier put me on a lead and then into a car. After a short journey, we stopped and the human took me out of the car and into a house. The humans had set up a dog bed, and they led me to it. It was a huge basket with a soft, fluffy quilt. I recognised it straight away – it was my bed. Looked like I was on to home number seven. I was used to this kind of change, so I didn't give it much thought. Anyway, as I might have mentioned, I like my bed. I lay down with one eye open so I could watch what was going on.

My new humans were called Adrian and Nicole.

There were two other dogs; their beds were either side of me. One was the big black and white dog called George that I knew from DogiPlayce. The other was a small terrier type that looked like a teddy bear. She was called Maxi. I had seen her around DogiPlayce, too, but she tended to keep to herself.

I lay there and waited.

It turned out that my previous owner had rehomed me here. She had also sent a long list of all my issues, over two pages neatly typed. I don't remember having issues. I don't remember a lot really – it's not what dogs do. If I think really hard, I can remember Bounce and I barking at passers-by, raiding the biscuit tin, things like that, but I don't consider those to be issues. Besides, Bounce did them, too, and he wasn't abandoned at DogiPlayce. Neither Adrian nor Nicole ever showed any indication that they had read this list. Maybe they threw it away.

That day, we three dogs were taken out for a couple of walks. The humans must have heard about my liking ball. Maybe Adrian had spotted this at DogiPlayce, because I got a lot of ball and I really liked that. That evening, I had my first dinner in my new home. Adrian and Nicole made us all sit and wait. I was quite happy with that. I like taking orders from humans, so I like being made to sit. The dinner itself was pretty good too – raw meat and biscuits. I love my food.

The next day we went out for a short walk before breakfast. When we got back, we had our breakfast and settled down for the day.

A routine was soon established. We had three or four walks a day: one before breakfast, one late at night before bed and the others during the day. I often got to play ball. Sometimes we walked around a field, and other times we

162

walked through the village. Sometimes, we'd meet other humans. I like other humans, and they seemed to sense that and I'd get pats. I do like getting attention, a lot.

I also like the routine.

What I like best of all is that Adrian and Nicole seem to understand dogs. I began to feel relaxed for the first time in a long time.

I hoped I'd be here a while.

George and I

My first proper introduction to George was when Adrian and Nicole took me into their house. George was there in his bed watching me being led in. George is one of the few dogs I have met who I didn't try to kill straight away – there was something about him. Humans can sometimes express leadership through displays of macho-type strength and bullying-type behaviours. Dogs express leadership through assertive yet calm, almost meditative behaviour. George just radiated strength combined with gentleness. Despite my instinctive fear, I could tell George was not a threat. In fact, I quickly came to respect George; he's just a great dog.

George has been a huge influence on my life. I'd go so far as to say that if there was one thing that's really helped me, it has been George. From day one, George has been great with me. He's never aggressive and always tolerant. His calm nature has provided me with the stability I needed. The humans have been great, too, but I think I owe much of my rehabilitation down to George.

I can't point at any particular events or things he has done. It has just been his presence.

I soon found myself following him and taking his lead. For example, he loves the sheep and spends time grooming them. I was a little scared, but bit by bit I have grown comfortable around them. I have even tried grooming them once or twice. I'm not sure I got it right, though, as one of them biffed me when I tried to lick it.

These days, I tend to follow George around wherever he goes. He's even taught me the rudiments of being a guard dog, and I have even gained enough confidence, alongside George, to bark at the odd intruder.

Thanks, George.

Food

I do like my food and even though I am given enough to eat, I am always on the lookout for a bit more. For example, on our walks I always try to scavenge a bit of sheep poo. Actually, I am quite partial to all types of poo, but sheep poo is my favourite. Not long after moving to my new home, I was exploring the house looking for scraps on the floor when I came across the kitchen bin. It smelt interesting, so I pulled it over and hunted through it for scraps. I was excited to find the plastic wrapping that had contained our dinner and as it smelt of meat, I ate it. It also tasted of plastic, but there you go.

I rooted through the rest of the bin, but there wasn't much there that smelt edible. I left all the bits I didn't want scattered over the floor and went back to bed. The next day we went out for a short walk before breakfast. When we got back, all the scraps I'd left out had been tidied up. Oh well! We had our breakfast and settled down for the day.

Whenever I got the opportunity, in other words whenever Adrian and Nicole were elsewhere, I would root through the kitchen bin. I soon realised that Adrian and Nicole were not too keen on this. This was not because they caught me or anything like that; it was just that they started setting me puzzles. The first was a chair blocking access to the bin. I had to figure out how to get past the chair. It took me a while. We dogs, we're not like crows –

we can't work things out very easily. However, I managed to move the chair out of the way. This was not because I was trying to do that, it just so happened the chair moved as I tried to squeeze through a gap to get to the bin. I learnt that I could move chairs. Over time, these puzzles became more elaborate. Some would take me a few days to work out.

Then one day, the bin was behind a door. I never got that door open.

Truth be told, over time, I lost interest in the kitchen bin. When we moved to Scotland, the bin was once again behind a door, but Adrian and Nicole often forgot to shut it properly. Nevertheless, I never raided it. Nor did I check the counters for food. There is a room where Adrian and Nicole keep the dog biscuits and defrost our dinners, and the door is often open, but I never go in. I'm not quite sure what keeps me out; I just never go in.

I like to scavenge when I am out and about. As I mentioned, I am quite partial to sheep poo, but will take pretty much any poo I can find, including dog, cat and even fox poo. Ah, fox poo – I love rolling in fox poo. Well, I used to, but every time I rolled in fox poo, I ended up having a bath, which I hated. So I stopped rolling in fox poo.

Anyway, we have lots of sheep here, so I have access to a lot of sheep poo. I have noticed that, over time, Adrian and Nicole have come to block me from eating sheep poo. Well, they have blocked me from eating any poo actually. What this has taught me is that I need to scavenge when they are not looking. That's not too hard – they are often distracted by the sheep, and that gives me a chance to grab a couple of pieces. Sometimes I eat too much and have to have a poo in the night, next to my bed.

Aside from that, I am happy with my two meals a day, though lately there seems to be a bit less meat than there used to be. That said, I feel a bit lighter and I'm able to run about more freely.

Other Dogs

I am deeply distrustful, even afraid of other dogs. I don't know why; I just feel very threatened when I see one. What I tend to do when a dog comes close is growl menacingly. If that doesn't scare it away, I charge it and bite it, snarling at the same time. It's only for a second or two, and we can be buddies afterwards. This used to cause problems with humans, and I could get punished. I never understood why – I was just trying to keep a threatening dog under control before it attacked me.

What I found in this new home with Adrian and Nicole is that they handled things differently. If they saw a dog coming towards us, I would be made to lie down on my side. Humans with dogs always seem to gravitate to each other for a chat, so this happened from time to time. It was pretty much always Adrian that had me on the lead. As I lay there getting more and more tense, he'd kneel down beside me. If I growled, he'd give me a sharp nudge and maybe a verbal warning. If I stayed quiet, he'd stroke my head. Most of the time nothing else would happen, and the other dog and human would head off.

The funny thing is, we used to go to DogiPlayce three mornings a week. Adrian worked there. It's how he'd found me. So, three times a week I'd meet loads of dogs, and nothing bad ever happened. I'd growl on the way in – sure enough, paying no attention to Adrian's attempts to stop me. But only for a second or two. Once I'd stopped growling, I just wandered off and found a spot to lie down. I'd soon settle and once settled, I found that I didn't really mind the other dogs. I also found that I since I had moved to my new home, I was no longer wearing a muzzle.

One day, we stopped going to DogiPlayce. I didn't miss

it much. However, we started going on long bike rides instead. What I mean by that is Adrian would cycle along, and George and I would have to trot alongside. I quite enjoyed that. I think George found it harder than me as he kept wanting to stop and check out smells. Adrian wouldn't allow this; we had to keep moving. Eventually, we'd get to a place where we were allowed to roam freely. It was a network of muddy tracks that passed between fields full of sheep and cows. Adrian would speed up and if we stopped, we'd have to run hard to catch up. Then we'd do it all in reverse till we were home again. It was brilliant fun but also pretty tiring.

One day, we came around a corner to see a female human approaching with a dog. As usual, Adrian was ahead; George and I had quite a slow trot and tended to lag behind a bit. By the time we got around that corner and saw the approaching human and dog, Adrian had dismounted and was waiting for us. He called George and I over and put us in a sit. I was then told to "relax", which I had learnt to mean lie down on my side with my legs stretched out.

I was reluctant to do this as a dangerous dog was approaching. However, I found myself lying on my side a few moments later. As the human and dog approached, I could hear Adrian chatting in human to the stranger. I could smell the strange dog. I growled, and Adrian nudged me on the neck. He did this with his hand, shaped like a dog's mouth. It made sense – it's what a parent dog would do to a misbehaving puppy. As such, it tapped into some deep-rooted instinct in me. I stopped growling and the next thing, I was getting a pat on my head.

I growled again, and got nudged again. I stopped growling, and got patted again.

This continued for a minute or so before I was let up to meet the strange dog. By now, George had already said hello. I got up and sniffed it. It seemed a little afraid of me. I looked up at Adrian as I wondered if we were going to continue the bike ride. As I did that, the strange human leant over and patted my head. I liked that. I wagged my tail vigorously.

Soon after, we were on our way again.

We'd occasionally meet dogs on those outings. If that happened, Adrian would always stop and have me in a relaxed position before the other dog got close. It kept me out of trouble, I suppose. By that, I mean there were no dog fights. I also got more attention from other humans than I'd ever had before. That was great.

I remember once we went on a town walk. We were in quite a large town and Adrian took George and me to a park. There were lots of strange humans and dogs here, and I wasn't quite sure what to make of it. George and I were on leads. George whimpered a lot. I think he wanted to go and play. I, however, was on high alert.

Adrian walked us amongst these dogs and kept George and I under control. I am not quite sure how, but we both found ourselves walking to heel. Eventually, we sat down. At one point, a stranger with a Labrador approached and started chatting to Adrian. I was about to send them packing but once again found myself in the "relax position". When I was allowed up again, all my fear and aggression had gone, and for a moment I was quite keen to meet this new dog. In the event, I sniffed the Labrador for a moment or two before lying down again.

However, even now and after many such meetings, I am still wary of other dogs. Once, I heard our human neighbours out in their garden and went over to see if they would play ball. I spotted a tiny terrier but, after a quick glance, I ignored it and went looking for a ball. On another occasion, I heard the same neighbours, went over and there was a different, strange dog there. I told that one off.

The only strange dog that I am OK with is the collie, Madge, that lives nearby. We often play ball together. There was a bit of a commotion when we first met. Adrian was talking to Madge's human, and I was sitting by Adrian's side. I saw Madge approaching and charged at her, growling. Next thing I found myself on my side in the "relax position". Madge sniffed me for a few moments before I was let up again. But we were fine after that.

Usually when there's a strange dog around, Adrian and Nicole stop anything getting out of hand. It doesn't happen very often, but I think that's because we live in quite a remote place.

Ball

While I like my bed and love my food, I live for ball. Ball is where a human throws a ball, then I run after it, catch it and take it back. This goes on until I am ready to drop. That's ball. There's nothing quite like ball. I love it. It's my favourite thing in the whole world. I can't get enough of it. I feel alive and vibrant when chasing that ball. Running after that ball, trying to snatch it as it bounces along, veering this way and that, it's just so amazing. Ball is even more important than food or pats – it's what I live for.

Ball!

When I am outside in the garden area, I will look for a ball. Once I have found one, I'll look for a human, trot over to said human, drop the ball in front of them, take two steps back and look up expectantly. Hopefully, the human will pick up the ball and throw it. If they don't, I pick up the ball and drop it again. And again. And again.

If they do throw it, I chase after it, catch it and take it back so I can drop it in front of them again. I'm pretty patient; I'll just keep dropping it till they throw it.

It doesn't matter what the human is doing. If, for example, they are sitting in a chair reading a book, I'll drop the ball in their lap. If they are in a sheep pen treating a sheep, I'll squeeze my jaws through a gap and drop the ball into the pen. Whatever they are doing, I'll find a way to drop the ball. Adrian and Nicole call this "inappropriate ball dropping". Apparently, I once dropped the ball in the middle of a pen where a sheep was having an operation. Well, I didn't know – I just wanted to play ball.

Madge does this, too, and sometimes, when we are both out, we team up. I like playing ball with Madge. She's a bit faster than me, so she usually gets to the ball first. She brings it back but not all the way, dropping it short. I then pick it up and take it back to the human. It works brilliantly.

I used to do this on walks, too. If, when we set off, I saw the human pick up a ball, I got really excited. Sometimes the human tried to hide the ball, but I knew it was there. I could smell it. Ball became all I thought about, and I would spend the whole walk running forward a few steps, stopping and then looking at the human expectantly. When they caught up, I would do the same again, and again, and again. Normally what happened was that we played ball for part of the walk, usually where it was open ground. Nevertheless, I spent the whole walk thinking "ball".

Of course, it's not quite as simple as that with Adrian and Nicole. These days we generally set off on a walk with no ball. If I then find one and drop it in front of them, the ball disappears. That's always perplexing as well as being disappointing. So, over time, I have learnt not to do this. The funny thing is that on walks I have, with experience, come to learn that not hoping for ball lets me get in touch with my inner dog and frees me up to go exploring interesting smells with George.

Nicole and Adrian keep a ball and ball launcher hanging in the porch, and I often gaze at it wistfully. However, they never seem to notice. In fact, over time, I have come to learn that begging to play ball with Adrian or Nicole never works. I have got used to that, even become OK with it, because, in a way, it means I can forget about ball and enjoy the moment. Strangely, it takes a lot of pressure off me and

I feel more relaxed generally. Don't worry, I do get ball. I just get it at Adrian and Nicole's convenience. Given that I like routine and I know I will get ball at some point, I don't spend the rest of the day worrying about not getting ball.

That said, ball! It's what I live for.

Sheep

Soon after I moved into Adrian and Nicole's house, they introduced me to some woolly creatures called "sheep". I looked at these sheep and felt like there was something I was supposed to be doing. I was off lead, so I was free to act. I tried to round them up but, I'll be honest, it was a bit of a half-hearted effort. Although I felt that I should be rounding them up, it wasn't much fun. My mind was more on ball. On top of that, the sheep didn't move. They just stood and looked at me. I doubled back and tried again. One of the sheep moved forward and tried to biff me. I managed to get out of the way in time, but decided rounding them up was too much trouble. I went over to Nicole and sat at her feet. I checked to see if she had a ball with her but couldn't see one.

That initial experience left me a little scared of sheep. We'd often pass through our sheep on one of our walks, but I tended to give them a wide berth. This was one area I was not too keen to follow George's example. He would be in amongst them trying to groom them or lick their bottoms clean. Some of the sheep seemed to like George, others would shoo him away, but George was always patient, almost deferential to the sheep.

Me, I kept my distance.

When we moved to Scotland, we had much more outdoor space and even more sheep. George and I would often be taken out when Adrian or Nicole were checking on the sheep. Our walks often passed through the sheep.

Bit by bit, I started to edge closer. At the same time, the sheep seemed to become more accepting of me. One day I tried licking one of the sheep, and it let me. I was pleased. I like grooming George, so I also tried grooming the sheep. That said, I don't do it very often. I'm too lazy really and, as I think I mentioned, I once got biffed for my troubles.

As I have become more relaxed around them, I have reverted to my natural tendency to find some long grass and lie down for a quick nap.

On Reflection

Looking back, I think things happened in my early life that messed with my head. I can't remember what, but by the age of three I was a fearful and unbalanced dog. All those humans that I had lived with, they had all rejected me.

I have been with Adrian and Nicole for many years now. I feel really settled and content. Where we live, we have plenty of space. As I said, George has taught me a bit about being a guard dog, so sometimes I join in when he barks at vans, and I enjoy that.

Despite this, I still have my fear of strange dogs. It must be really deep-rooted; something bad must have happened when I was a puppy. My instinct is always to get my attack in first. Adrian has worked with me a lot on this, and I think I am better than I used to be, but it's hard for me to judge. Living here, I don't get to meet many strange dogs, so this problem is a rare occurrence. That said, we recently visited Kika's home and though we had met before, I had kind of forgotten. If it hadn't been for Adrian controlling the introductions, I would have gone for her. As it was, I just managed a couple of growls. I also went for a dog in a nearby park. My attack bark set off George and Kika, and all three of us would've piled in had Nicole not had us on a lead. I think, maybe, I still have a problem there.

As a collie I am a working dog, and my breed was created in order to round up sheep. I have found I am not really that interested in herding, but my working needs are satisfied by ball. In my life here I get enough ball, which means I can sleep contented at nights.

My humans have been good to me. They are strong but kind and provide good leadership. I am not a leader, so would hate to be put in that position. Here, I have my humans and I have George. George is the leader of all the dogs, so when there are no humans around, we follow George. By we, I mean myself and Madge.

I feel I have been lucky. I know my humans were not looking for another dog when they took me on. I think Adrian spotted me on my own at DogiPlayce that day and he was not happy about my situation. I think, that day, he sorted things out so I would never see my previous human again. I am very grateful for that. I needed stability, not uncertainty, at that time. He gave me my life back.

So, on reflection, I have had a great life here. Kitchen bins are a distant memory. It's just a good, relaxed house to live in. Just what I need.

Case Studies

I have included five case studies to give an insight into the challenges faced in rehabilitating dogs. The biggest challenge, as these case studies show, is the reluctance of dog owners to acknowledge that their dog's problem stems from their own behaviour. Some cannot even accept they own a problem dog. We have all seen it, the small yappy dog that lunges at anything that passes. That is a dog with a problem. However, I would fully expect that the owner would deny this and say something along the lines that the dog is feisty or has spirit. The reality is that it's a problem dog, and could be classed as a "dangerous dog" under the Dangerous Dogs Act (UK). Would we be so tolerant of a large dog acting in this way?

The vast majority of dogs' problems stem from their human owners. I have heard all sorts of things from owners in denial such as "he's a sensitive soul", "she just doesn't like loud noises", "she likes to follow me around all the time", "me and my baby, we can't be apart", "I can't separate them (the dogs) more than a few feet or they get anxious", and so on.

These are all human issues transferred onto the dogs. In human therapy, "transference" is the label given to a situation where feelings, desires and expectations of one person are redirected onto to another person. In dog ownership, these are transferred onto the dogs. With guidance and help, humans can understand transference and do something about it. Dogs cannot think like that. For dogs, transference can be a disaster.

Furthermore, in this day and age, people seem to want a quick fix for anything including, in my experience, "problem" dogs. Perhaps this desire is fuelled by TV programmes where a dog behaviourist visits a problem dog, makes a quick assessment, comes up with a simple approach and all is fixed. I do, as it happens, enjoy these TV programmes. The dog behaviour people clearly know their stuff. What I admire most is their skill in handling the owners and often, unknown to the owners, creating changes in the owners' behaviours. What I feel doesn't come across clearly enough is the owner agreeing to change the way they handle their dog going forward. The impression given is that the dog's problems have been resolved there and then. So, while these programmes are good entertainment, they can create a false impression and expectation. Dogs are not "fixed" in a single visit. They need lifelong changes in the behaviour of their owners.

Given that most dogs' problems originate with their owner, I find with my clients that I have to draw deeply on my training as a therapist (for people). Even with that, I often struggle to convince people that, in order to have a happy dog, they need to change themselves, not the dog.

Another contributory factor is the eternal greed of the corporate pet industry. How many dogs are now labelled "companion" breeds? That label is both simplistic and misguided. A dog's needs are far more complex than walks, treats, pats and comfortable beds to sleep on.

Dogs are working animals, and each breed has been bred to carry out specific tasks. They need to be able to carry out these tasks. How can a working dog that is not allowed to work be happy? Collies need to round things up. Guard dogs need something to guard. Retrievers need to retrieve. Hounds need to follow scents. Huskies need to pull sledges, and so on. Here, dogs and humans share a common need: if we cannot work, we can lose our sense of purpose and sink into depression. So it is with dogs.

Here are my stories. All names and places have been changed.

The Pit Bull Terrier and the Needy Lady

Susan was an elderly English lady who had recently returned from living abroad. Overseas, she had acquired a pit bull terrier called Jack, and she had brought him back with her. She had moved into a cottage in a small, rural village. The problem she had with Jack was that he would attack anything on four legs. When walking Jack, Susan was in a perpetual state of anxiety that she would meet other dogs or, worse, horses. It was getting to the point where Jack never went further than the garden gate.

When I first arrived at Susan's house and knocked on the door, Jack went into a frenzy. I could hear him bouncing around and as soon as the door was opened, he charged out and leapt up at me barking for all he was worth. I ignored him completely and stepped inside. As an "alpha dog", I was communicating with Jack, in "dog", that I was higher status, not a threat and not interested in all this jumping and barking. Susan, as with most of my clients, seemed a little perplexed with my behaviour and jumped to the conclusion that I didn't like dogs. She began to make excuses for him. I explained what was going on, but she didn't look convinced.

After a short chat, I took Jack out for a walk. I went on my own because, often in these cases, if the owner comes with me, their energy can affect the situation. As it turned out, Jack was an easy dog to walk. He trotted alongside me stopping occasionally to sniff something. Walking around a field, I let him onto a longer lead and he snuffled around as happy as can be. Both he and I were completely relaxed, the lead never needed to be tightened. When I saw another dog approaching, I did see Jack beginning to tense up, but it was a simple task to redirect Jack's attention away. The key point here is that I was controlling Jack mentally. I never needed to use physical strength.

Jack should have been an easy case.

Susan told me her story. She had returned from abroad because of unrequited love. She also had strained relationships with an ex-husband and children to deal with. She was not really in a good place.

From Jack's perspective, Susan was weak. This might sound simplistic, but dogs don't have the same relationship issues as humans. They don't care. They just need a decent pack leader to set the rules so they can relax and get on with being a dog. Susan was not a pack leader, so Jack had to step in. It was not Susan taking Jack for a walk; it was Jack taking Susan for a walk. It therefore fell to Jack to see off any potential dangers. That's bred into terriers – they are guard breeds as well as vermin control.

The role of pack leader is an important point because I have met many dog owners who readily accept that their dog rules the roost. "Ha ha, yes, it's my dog that takes me for a walk!" or "Ha ha, my dog is the boss round here!" are just a couple of things I often hear the owners say. Worse, they often seem proud of this fact. Actually, this is quite a serious issue and a failure on behalf of the owner to take their responsibilities as a dog owner seriously. Susan was one such owner and while recognising Jack's dominance, she nevertheless seemed unwilling to see it as a problem.

When I took Jack out, I was in charge and Jack was able to relax. His behaviour improved straight away. Yes, there were some learnt behavioural issues regarding approaching four-legged creatures, but nothing too serious. Susan even remarked that she used to look on in wonder from her window as I walked Jack. "You both look so relaxed," she kept telling me.

I explained to Susan how she needed to make some changes in how she looked after Jack. These included making Jack sit for his dinner, banning treats between meals (unless part of training) and not allowing Jack onto her bed or sofa without ensuring he had asked for permission first. I coached Susan on how to train Jack in making him sit or go into the "down" position. I also showed her how to control the door to avoid all that jumping and barking.

On dog walks, I coached Susan how to handle Jack when four-legged creatures came into view. This involved turning Jack away so he did not have direct line of sight, putting him in a "down" position and distracting him. Susan, herself, needed to be assertive, calm and relaxed. Susan saw this working on many occasions. For example, on one walk, three horses (with riders) suddenly came around the corner. I calmly put Jack into a down and rewarded him each time he looked away from the horses. The horses walked past without incident. Susan had seen that Jack was perfectly capable, with the right handling, of coping with four-legged creatures without any fuss.

Even with all this evidence, she never made any changes as far as I could see. Jack never sat for his dinner. Jack continued to attack the front door, sleep on the bed and jump on and off the sofas at will. In fact, I became an expensive dog walker and Susan's therapist. After walking Jack, we spent a lot of time talking about this man who was still, even now, dominating her life.

I was never able to convince Susan that, for Jack to improve, it was Susan who needed to change. An example which brought this to light was Jack sleeping on Susan's bed. To set the scene, Susan was adamant that Jack needed to sleep on her bed. She was convinced it was core to his well-being, because he would be miserable sleeping elsewhere.

One day, Susan went away for a week and left Jack at a dog care centre. When she came back, Jack chose to sleep on the landing. When Susan told me this, I asked whether this bothered her. She admitted that it did. I then asked Susan if Jack was happy sleeping on the landing, and Susan said that he seemed perfectly happy. So, here we had a situation which directly contradicted Susan's view that sleeping on her bed was core to Jack's well-being. Jack was "perfectly happy" sleeping elsewhere. This gave me an opening to address the elephant in the room. I asked Susan, given what was happening, whose need was being satisfied by Jack sleeping on her bed. Susan went very quiet. She never answered, but her eyes told me that I had finally got through; her failure to answer indicated that she did not want to accept this.

This is a classic example of a dog owner putting their needs before the dog. Susan had personal issues and needed love and companionship. She sought to fill this gap in her life with Jack. In so doing, Susan had created a set of needs for Jack, such as Jack needing to sleep on the bed, Jack needing to be on the sofa, and so on. This was Susan projecting her needs onto Jack. The reality was that Susan needed Jack to be on the sofa next to her; Susan needed Jack to sleep on her bed.

Susan reluctantly admitted that her fear was that if she changed the way she looked after Jack, then Jack would stop loving her. This is human logic, which bears no relation to how dogs think. However Susan behaved towards Jack, he would still have loved her unconditionally. The crux was that Susan chose to fulfil her human needs through Jack. Jack was her emotional crutch. Susan's real, unspoken fear was that any change would mean that Jack would no longer fulfil her needs.

Jack, as a dog, was ill-suited to this task. Jack, as a dog, felt he had to step up and protect this weak human and in so doing, he became pack leader. The problems arising in his behaviour were a direct result of Susan's behaviour. While Susan could understand this intellectually, her emotional state prevented her from making any changes to her own behaviour.

The responsibility of being pack leader over a "human pack" does not sit well with most dogs, and as such can create a whole set of unstable behaviours. Dogs are often unable to determine what, in a human world, is threatening and what is not, so they tend to defend their space and their humans inappropriately. This can be anything from barking to a full-on attack. Pit bull terriers like to use their mouths, so they are likely to bite. Aside from this being dangerous to other people and animals, the dog is likely to be stressed. Not all dogs make natural leaders.

Jack was actually quite a gentle dog. However, he had learnt that it was his responsibility to attack other four-legged creatures when out with Susan. His behaviour was entirely natural from a dog's point of view.

The fundamental problem I had in this case was my inability to find a way to help Susan understand, let alone admit, that it was her behaviour and her state of mind that led to Jack attacking these animals. I was never able to determine whether Susan actually did understand but couldn't, or even wouldn't, make any changes. Susan had seen me handling Jack and walking him near horses and other dogs without incident. She saw how relaxed both Jack and I were. She had seen what Jack was capable of. But she could not get past her own needs, so, sadly for Jack, things didn't change.

Two English Bull Terriers Trying to Kill Each Other

"I've just had to pay a vet bill for eight hundred pounds," Mark told me on the phone. "We have two English bull terriers and they keep fighting. One got hold of the other's neck and ripped it open. Can you help?"

English bull terriers are quite a formidable-looking breed, which I have generally found to be quite placid and gentle. However, like all dogs, in the wrong place with the wrong energy, they can do a lot of a damage. Mark's two were called Pickle and Jar. The situation was that Mark had had Pickle for a few years and he'd been advised to get him a companion. Asking around, he was told that another English bull terrier would be a good choice. I did some research and found numerous articles stating the contrary. In fact, the general advice was that two English bull terriers in the same house was asking for trouble. This illustrates one of the problems of the modern world; there is so much information available but much of is contradictory. Sometimes it's hard to know what to believe.

I arranged to drop by. Pickle and Jar lived in a hotel, so they not only had each other to contend with but numerous strange humans in their territory either sleeping over or hanging around the bar. A challenging environment for a guard/fighting breed.

When introducing a new dog into a house with a resident dog, the pack hierarchy is key. Wild dog packs do not readily accept newcomers; they generally chase strange dogs away. The key is for the new dog to gain acceptance by the pack leader. Once this is achieved, the other dogs will follow the pack leader and accept the new dog. So, when introducing a new dog into your home, the new dog will likely be more easily accepted if you are the pack leader. However, if the resident dog is pack leader, then much will depend on the nature of the new dog. If the new dog is submissive, the introduction will probably go without incident. If the new dog is dominant, it will likely challenge the resident and you could have a dog fight on your hands. This is what was happening with Pickle and Jar. Jar was trying to take over, but Pickle was having none of it. Both were dominant dogs.

I met Pickle first. I took him outside onto the patio, leaving Mark and a small entourage that had come to watch inside. I needed to assess Pickle in a controlled environment. I did a simple exercise: I stopped Pickle from going back to the door. When he tried, I just blocked him with my legs. I started off with him on a lead (in case he got past), but I was soon able to let him free. It went on for a while. Pickle would look back at the door, try to go past me, find himself blocked, step back, look at me, look at the door, and so on.

This was a powerful exercise. I was teaching Pickle two lessons: First, I was higher status. Second, I was not a threat.

After 20 minutes or so, I was getting somewhere but then it started to rain. Straight away, I could see that Pickle did not like the rain. This was going to ruin the exercise. The last thing I needed was Pickle getting anxious. I put him back on the lead and headed back inside. Stepping through the door, I was met by a row of expectant faces, so I stopped and gently placed Pickle in a sit. I started to explain what I had been up to but soon realised that no one was listening. They were all looking at Pickle. I stopped talking.

"How did you do that?" one of them asked.

"Do what?" I replied.

"Get Pickle to be – well, to be like that," came the response. I looked down, and Pickle was sitting there quite happily, quite chilled. I have to admit that I was a bit puzzled; he seemed perfectly normal to me. It turned out they had never seen Pickle so relaxed and obedient. They couldn't believe what I had achieved in 20 minutes. I think that was a key moment insofar as Mark realised that I did know what I was doing. What he didn't realise was that I was only just getting started.

I also had to meet Jar. Jar was in a dog crate two floors up. Jar and Pickle were being kept at opposite ends of the property, fed at different times and walked separately. I went up, alone, to meet Jar. Jar watched me enter the room with that quizzical look common to dogs. That was excellent – curious, not aggressive. I sat down in front of the crate with my back to him for a few minutes. Nothing happened, so I got up, opened the crate door and waited. Jar looked at me and waited. I was pleased; no charging out was sign of respect for me. I brought Jar out and put him on a lead.

I had noticed on the way up that the stairs were narrow, old and uneven. Jar was a powerful dog so, for my own safety, I'd have to control him carefully coming down the stairs. The basic rule was that Jar had to walk behind me and if I stopped, he had to sit. While he was a quick learner and pretty responsive, it still took about 40 minutes to get down both flights of stairs. With dogs, you need to be really patient and do it absolutely correctly, as this taps into their way of thinking. It was 40 minutes well spent as I was later told that bringing Jar down the stairs had, before my visit, been a major problem, but after my visit it had become a joy.

The next task was to bring the dogs together. The best way to do this was on a walk. With them moving forward, they would be more inclined to bond and less inclined to attack each other. At this point, I was inside the door with Jar, and Mark was outside with Pickle. Jar was a bit too excited, so I sent Mark off ahead with Pickle. Once they'd gone about 20 metres, I set off with Jar and slowly caught up till Mark, Pickle, Jar and I were walking alongside each other. I was giving Mark a running commentary on what was going on, what to expect and how to react. Jar did show an inclination to go for Pickle, but the combination of a quick pace and a sharp, well-timed tug on the lead was enough to head off any problems.

While the walk went well and without incident, there was little evidence that Pickle and Jar had bonded. That said, at least they weren't tearing lumps out of each other. Jar was the root of the problem. He clearly wanted to be the alpha dog, so he was always looking for his chance to go for Pickle. I had to be alert to head him off. Jar was not too keen on this discipline, and eventually he lost it. He tried to get free, and then went into that dog frenzy of jumping, twisting, snarling and biting. Mark looked quite worried. I just told him to step back a little (with Pickle) and watch.

While Jar danced around like a rabid pogo stick, I chatted away to Mark about how this was fine, not to worry and that Jar would soon wear himself out. In fact, it was a good thing because Jar, having thrown everything at me, would now have no choice other than to submit. Sure enough, after a few minutes, Jar stopped and stood there panting. He was worn out. I rolled him onto his side and laid my hand on his chest. Jar had submitted.

We were then able to walk back to the hotel with two tired dogs.

Author's note: I should make it clear here that, while I might have made the above exercise sound easy, it was anything but. Going a bit "manic" is one of a number of possible natural reactions from a dog whose high status is challenged. It is the fight/flight response kicking in and, off lead, the dog would either run away or fight the "challenger" to maintain its dominant position. In this situation, I have to win, but I also have to avoid fighting as I could get injured and the dog could become frightened of me. Having a large, powerful, unmuzzled fighting dog in this frenzy with just a lead to control him is potentially quite dangerous. Nevertheless, dogs have evolved a complex "language" to deal with conflict, making fighting the last resort. The skill is allowing the dog to wear itself out while keeping out of range from the snapping jaws and at the same time remaining calm, almost meditative (this means I am perceived as strong but not threatening). This way, I prove I am stronger but, more importantly, by not harming or threatening the dog in any way, it will come to respect rather than fear me. Eventually, the dog will tire and submit. That said, even knowing what I was doing, I still had quite a few scratches on my arm afterwards.

The next step was indoor introductions. I brought Jar into the room first and laid him on his side. He was tired after his walk and therefore relaxed and amenable. Once I was happy that his energy was right, I asked Mark to bring in Pickle. Satisfied that they were both at "level zero" (calm), we let the dogs free. The key was to watch both dogs carefully and look out for one them starting to fixate on the other, as that could be the prelude to an attack. Predictably, it was not long before Jar tensed and looked fixedly at Pickle. I intercepted him with a quick nudge to the neck with my fingertips. This redirected his attention away from Pickle and onto me, thus defusing the situation long before it got out of hand. This action is similar to the nips puppies get from their mothers when they misbehave. Mark was able to see first-hand both the problem behaviour and the method of intervention.

Jar tensed up two or three more times, and this time Mark was able to intervene. I talked Mark through other situations to look out for. For example, Jar would get up on a chair and look down at Pickle – a dominant behaviour that could easily be viewed by Pickle as a challenge. Here, all Mark had to do was move Jar back onto the floor. After about five minutes, Pickle and Jar settled down. Pickle was the more relaxed of the two, probably because he was older. Jar was young and excitable, but he had settled as well. For the first time, Pickle and Jar were in close proximity and not tearing lumps out of each other. Mark was delighted.

This case shows what can be achieved when the dog owner is willing to take responsibility and make changes. Mark was certainly motivated by the huge vet bills, but he was also quite interested in learning to understand how dogs think and why they acted in certain ways. The result was that Mark put in place changes which made real differences to Pickle, Jar and Mark's family. They went from a highly stressful situation with two warring dogs back to normality with the two dogs wandering around peacefully.

Mark and the dogs did well.

Two Jack Russells Rule the Roost

I was contacted by two elderly ladies who were having problems controlling their dogs on walks, so I arranged a visit. On entering their house, I was met by two mini tornadoes. Two Jack Russell terriers clearly ruled this house and as they careered around the place leaping over sofas and tables, I stood there thinking it was a miracle that nothing was getting broken.

The dogs were called Maggie and Millie. Their owners were Mary and Ruth, both in their 70s. Someone had advised them that two high-energy Jack Russell terriers would be just the perfect dogs for them. I stood, somewhat in shock, as Mary and Ruth tried to gain some semblance of control. It was like watching tortoises trying to round up cats.

Snapping myself out of my reverie, I plucked one of the terriers out of the air as it passed by and placed it on its back. This might sound drastic, but I was copying behaviour I had observed in dogs. I once went on a walk with two German shepherds. One was mine (Shadow), and the other (Rex) belonged to another couple who joined us on the walk. Rex was manic, pretty much like Maggie and Millie. He had emerged from the car like a missile, charging around the car park scattering people and dogs alike, before running flat out straight into a tree. Undeterred, it had then started pestering Shadow. This involved stealing every twig Shadow picked up and generally being a nuisance. Shadow ignored Rex completely until he'd had enough. In a flash, he flipped Rex on his back, growled and planted a paw on his chest. It worked and the rest of the walk was quite peaceful.

I was using the same approach. Unfortunately, it didn't quite come off, and I now had a squirming, aggressive terrier (Maggie) pinned to the floor. This is one of the few dogs I have encountered that managed to sink its teeth into me. I adjusted my position and kept Maggie in place. This was going to be a challenge. Millie continued to hurtle around the room, but eventually curiosity overcame exuberance and she came to investigate what I was doing. I ignored her completely. Eventually, Maggie relaxed and submitted, and I let her go.

Turning my attention to Mary and Ruth, I started chatting about the dogs, how they came to have them and why they wanted them. All the time, Maggie and Millie bounced around the room like whirling dervishes. Conversation was proving tricky. It was just mad.

Sometimes you get a feeling that you are not going to be able to help. These two dogs were totally unsuitable for Mary and Ruth. Not only did they know next to nothing about dogs, they showed little inclination to learn. Furthermore, I had the impression that they thought I was going to perform some kind of miracle and "fix" the dogs. But the solution was going to require Mary and Ruth to make changes, not the dogs. Attempts to explain this were met with blank looks of incomprehension.

This illustrates a common issue. People are generally well-meaning and they think their dogs are happy. When their dogs show odd behaviours, they will likely say that it's the dog "being sensitive" or words to that effect. These people consistently fail to acknowledge the link between their own behaviours and their dogs' problems. They are deaf to any notion that they themselves might be the root of the problem. So it was with Mary and Ruth.

Nevertheless, I tried.

What I really needed to do was separate the dogs from each other and from their owners. I needed to work with each dog individually to establish my status and to set some ground rules. I needed Mary and Ruth out of sight and out of mind so the dogs had only me to deal with. Mary and Ruth did not like this idea. They insisted on watching what I was doing. I was not getting anywhere, so I just made myself comfortable and chatted to Mary and Ruth.

I talked about dog psychology, including dominance and hierarchies. I explained to Mary and Ruth they had to be in charge and that the only way they could control these dogs was through the dogs' minds. I also explained that Jack Russells were a pretty challenging breed, highly independent and not easy to handle. I talked about training and how to teach dogs simple commands such as "sit" and "down". There were lots of enthusiastic nods accompanied by puzzled expressions.

I realised how impossible this task was going to be when I demonstrated how to control the walk.

A dog's walk begins in the house. The trick is to keep control from the moment you decide to go out, which means the dog must remain calm during the pre-walk preparation. No dancing around in joy as you fetch the lead. No straining to get out through the door. No bouncing around like manic grasshoppers. Calm!

Mary and Ruth had developed a ritual for putting the dogs on their leads. It was quite a show. Maggie and Millie, having seen Mary fetch the leads, were now bounding around the kitchen in a frenzy of excitement. Somehow, Mary attached leads to them both. I took both leads, walked the dogs a few metres away from the door and stopped, stood still and waited. I explained to Mary and Ruth that, if we left the house with dogs in this excitable state, we were asking for trouble. They told me it was always like this. I explained that the key was starting the walk as you meant it to go on: calm and relaxed. I told them that if they followed my advice, the walks would get better.

Maggie and Millie were still highly excitable, so I ignored them while waiting for them to calm down. I carried on talking to Mary and Ruth explaining what was going on and why I was doing what I was doing. Maggie and Millie finally registered that nothing was happening; they stopped wriggling and looked up at me expectantly. Now I had their attention, I moved towards the door. As I had expected, this set them off, so I returned to the original position and turned my attention back to Mary and Ruth. All the time Millie and Maggie were acting up, I simply pretended they didn't exist. They had to learn that to get my attention and to get what they wanted, they had to calm down and show me some respect.

It took me a good 20 minutes but finally there I was standing at an open door with two calm, sitting Jack Russells. I explained that, over time, the dogs would learn this new approach and that this would in turn make everything easier. I also tried to reinforce the point that my control had been entirely via the mind. I had not used any physical force or any vocal command at any stage of this process. I had thought (but not stated out loud) that Mary and Ruth, being retired, would have the time to do this themselves. However, I could see from the looks on their faces that they were somewhat horrified at the prospect.

The walk was a great success and enjoyed by all five of us. Maggie and Millie were a little excitable but responsive. I had no problem controlling them. Mary and Ruth had seen what was possible.

Before I left, I tried one more time to explain that dogs needed to be treated as dogs and that the best way to turn them into good pets was through the application of dog psychology. Understand the dogs' needs and then put in place measures to satisfy those needs, and you will have a happy, obedient dog. However, I was not convinced that they agreed with me.

Mary and Ruth were elderly ladies who enjoyed sitting in the garden and going on short walks. They had sought companion dogs with which, in their imagination, they would spend peaceful time sharing these activities. Mary and Ruth were convinced they had the right dogs because that's what they had been told. They showed little or no interest in seeing the situation from the dogs' point of view.

As far as they were concerned, they were good owners and the problem was all down to the dogs. They saw no reason to change what they were doing.

This case study illustrates a common issue in dog ownership: a failure of the owner to take any responsibility for the problems arising. Their dogs had the best beds, the best food and unlimited love and attention. Mary and Ruth treated these terriers as grandchildren and spoilt them. The terriers had responded by taking over and doing exactly as they pleased. As far as Mary and Ruth were concerned, they were "doing everything right". The fact that Maggie and Millie were a bit of a nightmare was an inconvenient truth. They were hoping for a quick TV-style fix that somehow flicked a switch inside their dogs and turned them into beautifully behaved little pooches. No amount of evidence could convince them that their dogs' errant behaviour was actually down to them.

Mary and Ruth recognised they had a problem and so had asked for my help. While their stated problem was in keeping the dogs under control on walks, the actual problem was that they had no control over the dogs at all. On top of this, Maggie and Millie had energy to burn and were, essentially, bored. Had Mary and Ruth been prepared to listen and make changes, we could have resolved their problems. As well as gaining control of Maggie and Millie, we could have devised "dog games" that would have been straightforward for Mary and Ruth to set up and be stimulating for the dogs. That way, they could have helped Maggie and Millie burn off their abundant energy and wear themselves out. A tired dog is much easier to handle.

Sadly, it was not to be.

The English Mastiff That Ate the House

I got a call from a lady who told me that she had acquired an English mastiff and it was eating the house. Was there anything I could do? I arranged to pop round.

Brenda lived in a small semi-detached house which she shared with her dachshund, Tinkle, and her recent acquisition, a male English mastiff puppy called Max. He might have been a puppy, but he was already huge and dominated the small living room. The house stank of dog. The furniture all showed signs of chewing. Brenda showed me around introducing me to a cluttered kitchen, another room with chewed books strewn across the floor and a tiny garden covered in dog poo.

We returned to the living room and sat down. Tinkle eyed me malevolently. Max lay behind the sofa contentedly chewing an unknown object.

Brenda told me her story. She was an accountant but had been on long-term sick leave for some time. She was suffering from clinical depression, and she showed me the drugs she was taking. She explained that she had owned Tinkle for years now and that Tinkle was really important to her. I asked why she had got Max. She told me about a time, when she was younger, when the family had owned an English mastiff. These had been happy times for her, so she had thought that bringing an English mastiff back into her life would rekindle this happiness. It had not occurred to her in her logic that she had not been responsible for looking after the mastiff during that time.

More to the point, it is a common failing that we humans often try to find happiness in the wrong places. We might seek people to make us happy or engage in activities such as retail therapy. The problem is, relying on other people or acquisitions to make us happy is fraught with pitfalls. The blues and despondency can soon return.

There are many good reasons for getting a dog, but

expecting it to cure clinical depression was a new one on me.

This was a complex situation and I needed time to think, so I took Max out for a walk. Max turned out to be a delightful dog. He was content, calm and attentive. He was also already so big and strong that it was like walking a small bull. Having owned cows, I have learnt that bulls can only be led – you cannot push them around. There was no way a dog like this could be controlled through physical strength.

On returning, I once again joined Brenda and Tinkle in the living room. Studying Tinkle, it was obvious, despite her size, that she was a highly dominant dog. She had as clear a case of "small dog syndrome" that I have ever seen. This is a condition that small dogs get when they are overindulged. They become spoilt, and their aggression is seen as amusing (rather than dangerous) and often encouraged. The picture of what was going on here was building up in my mind.

If Brenda were to indulge Max in the same way as she did Tinkle, there was a risk that she could create a monster.

I asked Brenda a few questions about Tinkle, how she looked after her, how she was on walks, and so on. This gave me the opening to discuss dogs with her. I explained that dogs did not think like humans. I talked about dogs and packs and pack leaders. I told Brenda that with a dog like Max, she absolutely had to be the pack leader. However, this would mean that she would have to change the way she handled Tinkle too. I also explained that the dogs would see her depression as a weakness. They would not care why she was like that; they would only care about her emotional state in the moment. Max was still a puppy, but when he came of age, he would probably want to take over.

As was often the case when speaking to clients about such matters, I felt Brenda understood me intellectually, but emotionally she saw things differently. She liked her relationship with Tinkle exactly as it was and Max was there to solve her problems, not the other way around.

This was potentially a catastrophe in the making, and I came to the conclusion that there was only one solution here: I had to persuade Brenda to rehome Max. This was the only time in my career as a dog behaviourist that I have had to make such a call. I realised it was not going to be easy. Max was a purebred puppy, so had cost Brenda a lot of money. She viewed him as the answer to her problems, and was convinced that Max was going to make her happy again. Having, as a hypnotherapist, worked with a number of clients suffering depression, I understand, up to a point, how the depressed mind works. I have also read a lot of books about depression. Bearing this in mind, I knew I would have to be careful how I put this suggestion across.

Falling back on my experience as a therapist, I focused on listening. I encouraged Brenda to talk about her future with Max. As she talked, I gently questioned how Max could fulfil such complex human needs. I planted suggestions about the level of care such a dog would need. As the discussion drew to a close, I sensed that Brenda remained resistant to the idea of rehoming Max. It was already a pretty dire situation, and Brenda failed to see that things would probably only get worse.

I was left with no option but to play my trump card. I asked how she would feel when Max killed Tinkle. Brenda looked at me with a horrified expression. I explained that this could go one of two ways. The first was that as Max grew from a puppy into a dog, he would probably challenge Tinkle for control of the pack. I told Brenda, perhaps a little bluntly, that Max could easily pick up Tinkle and snap her neck.

The second, and more likely outcome, would be that Tinkle would go for Max. It was clear to me that Tinkle resented this intruder in her space. I said that Max would probably try to step away and avoid a fight but, with him being so big and with the room so cluttered and small, there was a chance he would step on Tinkle and hurt her. Brenda looked at me and then told me quietly that this had already happened. Max had accidentally broken Tinkle's leg. It had cost her a fortune.

I felt I had made my case, so I turned the conversation over to what would happen next. I agreed to come back in a couple of weeks and see how things were.

No sooner had I got home than I found a message on the phone. Brenda had checked herself into hospital, and in the message she asked if I would go round and feed her dogs for her. She had left a key with a neighbour. Brenda was unreachable. I rang the RSPCA for advice. They said they couldn't intervene as it was not a clear case of animal cruelty. I got the feeling they were batting it back to me. I didn't feel that I had any choice other than to step in and help. The dogs' welfare was the primary issue.

So, I rang around some dog people I knew and managed to arrange for some help. I went over in the afternoons, walked the dogs, fed them and cleaned up some of the dog mess. One of my colleagues went over late at night to check on them and another first thing in the morning. I think someone even stayed over one night.

After three days, Brenda returned but seemed unaware and disinterested in the crisis she had caused. The only thing that got her attention was my bill. I reiterated that she needed to rehome Max and work with her doctor to deal with her depression.

I heard soon after, via a friend of a friend, that Brenda had rehomed Max. I was more than relieved. Brenda would be fine with Tinkle. Tinkle might have made a case study in her own right but so far as Brenda was concerned, Tinkle was perfect. I felt a little sorry for Tinkle, but there was nothing I could do about it.

This case highlights one of the big problems faced by dogs. People get a dog for all the wrong reasons. Owning a dog brings with it responsibility – the primary responsibility being meeting your dog's needs. It's not the other way around. Getting a dog to fill a hole in your life is an irresponsible act.

If you want to get a dog, think carefully about your reasons and make sure they are good ones. Time spent researching breeds is time well spent. I would also suggest thinking carefully before acquiring a purebred dog as these often come with all sorts of issues – physical as well as mental. Most of all, remember that dogs are working animals and that working is a core need. A dog chosen for the right reasons and looked after correctly is a brilliant companion. They are not, ever, a solution for your problems.

The Malamute and the Cat

This was one of my first cases. It involved a Malamute that was getting into fights with the resident cat, usually at meal times. The owners asked for my help.

My first impression on entering the living room was that this was an easy dog. There was none of the excitable jumping around that I often encounter when meeting new dogs. The Malamute, Henry, just wandered over and sniffed my leg. The owners (Jill and Cliff) and I sat down and they explained what was going on. It was a classic case of dog and cat not getting on.

Dogs and cats are predators, and predators are programmed to eliminate other predators on their patch. You just have to watch a few nature programmes to see this. Examples include leopards living in trees to keep themselves safe from lions, cheetahs keeping a wide berth from bigger predators, and smaller predators sneaking around trying to remain undetected. Different types of predators just don't mix. Cats and dogs are not natural companions.

How they interact will, by and large, depend on their environment when they are very young. Dogs born and bred in houses with cats will have grown up with cats from such an early age that the dogs will view cats as funny-shaped dogs. The same is true the other way around. However, cats and dogs more often get to meet each other once they are a bit older.

It's also worth noting that in many dog and cat houses, the cat establishes itself as higher status. This actually leads to less conflict as the dog will naturally give way. However, it is in many dogs' nature to chase cats, whatever status they might have.

When cats and dogs in a home don't get on, the trick is to introduce them carefully and enable them to relax in each other's company. This can be reinforced with rewards. I got

Henry to relax at my feet. It only took a few minutes. As I said, he was quite an easy dog. Nevertheless, Jill and Cliff were surprised at how easy I had made it look. I explained all about being relaxed, assertive and non-threatening, and how dogs responded to that. I sent Jill and Cliff to fetch the cat. Cats being cats, I asked for it to be put into its carry basket. When they brought the cat in, I had them set it down a little way away from Henry with the door facing away. Henry tried to raise his head to look, but I gently pushed it back down. When he stopped, I stroked his head.

The cat was spitting and howling a little but soon settled down. In stages, we brought the cat closer until it was next to Henry with the door facing Henry. They could see each other. All the time, the atmosphere was calm and relaxed. I suggested to Jill and Cliff that they carried out this exercise daily until such a time as the relationship improved to where they wanted it to be. I explained that we were basically teaching them both to be relaxed and non-threatening in each other's company.

Jill and Cliff had mentioned issues at meal times, so I asked to see where they were fed. It was obvious to me what the problem was here. Henry's bowl was very close to the cat flap. If Henry was eating, the cat would have to force its way past Henry in order to use the cat flap. If Henry was not eating, the cat would have to approach Henry's bowl. Henry might view that as the cat stealing his food. I suggested a different place for the dog bowl.

This was an easy case study requiring only one visit. The dog and cat were both pretty chilled to start with, and it just needed a gentle nudge and change of feeding arrangements to bring peace and harmony. Also, Jill and Cliff were happy to spend a little time helping Henry and the cat get used to each other's company. That's sometimes all it takes – a little time and willingness to act.

Glossary

Balanced Dog   A dog that is content with life has a generally calm disposition and does not exhibit behaviours such as being yappy, clingy, aggressive, depressed or anxious.

Discipline   A set of rules adopted by a pack of dogs – not to be confused with punishment. Discipline provides the cohesion that holds the pack together.

Level 0 to 10   Level 0 is a calm, relaxed dog. Level 10 is a super excited or aggressive dog – in human terms, a dog that has "lost the plot".

Pack Leader   The alpha dog in the pack. This dog makes the decisions such as where to go each day in search of food. Note that dogs will only follow a balanced leader, so the pack leader must exhibit the qualities of calmness and assertiveness. In a human household, the humans form part of the pack.

Relax Position	This is the dog lying on its side with its legs stretched out as though it is lying in front of the fire.
Separation Anxiety	An anxious state of mind experienced by some pet dogs when their owners leave them on their own.
Submit	By submitting, a dog is accepting your higher status and letting you know that it is doing so.
Transference	When humans transfer their feelings, desires and needs onto another person or, in the case of this book, a dog.
Weak	Humans often measure strength as physical or mental dominance. In dogs, strength is akin to inner strength and projecting power through gentleness. Dogs perceive humans as weak if they are angry, depressed, unhappy or unwell – pretty much anything except assertive, calm and relaxed.

Acknowledgements

I would like to say an enormous thank you to my wife, Nicole, for her enthusiasm and encouragement and, of course, her diplomatic feedback on each of the developing drafts. I also owe thanks to Matt Lamb and Elizabeth Conte-Rigg for providing valuable feedback and, of course, my editor Alex for her painstaking work in improving overall readability. Thanks also to Matt Lamb for his superb cover design. And, of course, my thanks to the four dogs whose stories form the basis of this book.

Printed in Great Britain
by Amazon